SOUND FAMILIAR?

"I just met this terrific man. We might actually have a chance together. What can I do this time to make sure it lasts?"

"I want sex with you twice a day because I love you so much."

"I get really scared if I start to feel good in a relationship."

"We've been together so long there aren't any surprises left."

"I love you so much that I'm going to buy you all this beautiful underwear to inspire you to lose weight. Then you'll be the same girl I married."

All these statements are cries of distress . . . made by people who don't know how to fulfill their own and their partners' need for intimacy.

Why does it seem so difficult to create a lasting love? Why do we sometimes sabotage our most important relationship? Dr. Crowther gives you the startling answers and the tools to meet the challenge. You can make love the ultimate experience and transform your life with . . .

INTIMACY

INTIMACY

*STRATEGIES
FOR
SUCCESSFUL
RELATIONSHIPS*

C. EDWARD CROWTHER, PH.D.
with
GAYLE STONE

A DELL BOOK

Published by
Dell Publishing
a division of
The Bantam Doubleday Dell Publishing Group, Inc.
666 Fifth Avenue
New York, New York 10103

Reprinted by arrangement with Capra Press

The trademark Dell® is registered in the U.S. Patent
and Trademark Office.

ISBN: 0-440-20012-1

Printed in the United States of America
Published simultaneously in Canada
June 1988
10 9 8 7 6 5 4
KRI

For my wife, Ingrid,
with whom the art of intimacy
is a way of life.

CONTENTS

CHAPTER 1

INTIMACY:
THE ELUSIVE QUEST

> The living mystery of life is always hidden between two, and
> it is the true mystery which cannot be betrayed by words and
> depleted by argument.
>
> —C.G. JUNG
> Letter, August 12, 1960
> *Collected Letters*

"I'm lonely." The young, attractive woman sat in my office. "We're a big family, but everyone's busy. It's the same way where I work. I have good friends I see now and then, and I've dated several men in the last few months, one steadily. But I don't feel really close to him, or to anyone for that matter."

This intelligent, friendly woman is caught in a situation that has happened to most of us—we're surrounded by people, yet we feel deeply alone. Being alone in a crowd really hurts.

But already this young woman senses the heart of her problem, and the problem's solution. She expresses it in her desire to "feel really close." Unconsciously, she's searching for intimacy. Despite the wealth of material satisfactions provided by today's high-tech world, the very human need for intimacy cries out even more. How we want it! How we need it! And when we say that, we're being really honest. We want it more than a million dollars, more than a Rolls Royce, more than status, more than power—more than anything, we want and need intimacy. The good news is that every man and woman, whether rich or poor, young or old, outgoing or a "loner," can create and sustain intimate relationships. From the innocent warmth of close childhood friendships to the long-lasting sexual love of marriage, we can have whatever we want from the wide spectrum of possibilities for intimacy in our lives.

Why? Because we're all born with the ability to be intimate. It's that simple.

* * *

Intimacy is our genetic, emotional drive to become fully human.

Intimacy at the emotional and spiritual level equals our physical needs for air, water, food, shelter, and sleep. Those are the only real needs the body has. Everything else is a 'want,' and we translate 'want' very quickly into 'need.' But when we say we need food, we really do need food or we will die.

Likewise we also need air, water, shelter, and sleep. That is all true. And at the same time I will add that I need—and you need— each one of us needs intimacy in our emotional and spiritual lives. Without it, our bodies can survive, but we cannot truly live.

But intimacy is elusive. Too many of us lead lonely, unfulfilling lives.

The highly developed society that has provided us with the luxuries of refrigerators, televisions, and jet travel cannot give us intimacy. In fact, our society often works inadvertently against deep, meaningful relationships by stressing other values, such as producing and consuming goods.

Advertisements bombard us with the message that ownership means happiness. Job advancement comes because we're good workers, and few people at the office or factory know or care whether we love our families or have personal problems or victories. It's no wonder that somewhere in our busy lives we begin to lose touch with our need for intimacy, and with our natural ability to have the intimate relationships we increasingly long for.

* * *

Several years ago I grew very fond of a man I knew who was dying of cancer. Let's call him Jerry. I went to see Jerry day after day at the hospital, and I was with him when he died because I had promised him I would be. Jerry was a very successful man who had built a small manufacturing business into an international corporation. He was in his early forties and extremely wealthy. He had thought he had everything.

Then he became ill with what his doctors diagnosed as a rapid-growing lethal cancer.

"You know," he told me in the hospital, "I let my wife slip away two years ago. I hadn't paid much attention to her for a long time, so when she wanted a divorce, I let the lawyers handle it. Then when I knew I had cancer, I did something I'd wanted to do for a whole year. I called her in Chicago. After the divorce, she moved there with our daughter. She said, 'I wish you'd called me a couple of weeks ago, Jerry, because last week I married again. Yes, I've also thought a lot about what went wrong in our marriage, but I wasn't prepared to put up with it any longer, or to wait for you. So I married again. I'm terribly sorry you've got cancer, but I can't have any part in this now. I have another life.' "

My friend Jerry lay quietly on his hospital bed, then he continued. "The only women in my life now are the nurses. They're very kind to me. Every morning I arrange to have roses sent to my nurses." He looked at me. "Because of my business, I had friends. But they're busy, working to get ahead just like I used to. You're the only person who still visits me. Do you think it's too late for you and me to develop a real intimate relationship?"

I learned a lot about the meaning of intimacy from Jerry, who had three weeks to live and wanted to strike up an intimate relationship with me. It was a relationship that didn't involve our bodies except that I held him as he was dying, and I wiped his face, and when he died I kissed him. He said to me, "I love you, baby." And I said, "I love you, too." He was the first man I'd ever said that to. He wasn't the last, but he was the first.

During our visits I felt able to tell him anything about who I was and who I wanted to be. I felt more freedom with Jerry than with any other living person up to that time. And he told me everything, too, sometimes things he was discovering for the first time simply because he was talking and revealing himself, allowing himself to be vulnerable.

At the end, we said our prayers together. I put on my bishop's hat and I laid him to rest. I think his soul does rest in peace, and I will always cherish him, my memories of him, and the illuminating relationship we grew together.

* * *

No one in the world is more honest than a person who knows death is near. The subterfuges and pretenses of life fall away, and the material aims for which each has spent a lifetime struggling become meaningless. Many are left instead with a shining, courageous honesty.

About ten years ago I conducted a study of people who were dying in hospices and orthodox hospitals in the United States and England. It was entitled *Care Versus Cure in the Treatment of the Dying.* I talked at length to each of the almost two hundred people in my statistical population sample. They were open and kind with me, and I was very grateful for their time.

When I asked each person individually what mattered most in life, around ninety percent answered intimate relationships. Many also added wistfully they wished they could impress the importance of these kinds of relationships on those they were leaving behind. A fifty-year-old mother of three children who was dying of cancer put it this way: "You need not wait until you are in my condition to know nothing in life is as important as loving relationships."

In my practice of psychotherapy, I see many, many people every year. Most have symptoms such as anxiety or depression, or they are beset with behavioral disorders such as overindulgence in drugs, alcohol, food, or work.

Increasingly I'm finding the absence of intimacy is the common denominator in the analysis and treatment of people with these and many other symptoms.

* * *

"We are the authors of all coming evil," Carl Jung said in a BBC television interview shortly before his death. "Yet we know practically nothing about man."

The greatest mystery of mankind is ourselves. In schools, we learn how to read and write, add and subtract, and, along the way, we acquire an array of intellectual tools to help us achieve in life whatever goals we choose. At home and in schools, we learn how to exercise, feed ourselves nutritiously, sleep regularly, and generally maintain strong, fit bodies.

Most of us assume that with these skills we will grow up to be normal, happy adults. In the traditional formula, we will date, find work, and marry. We will advance in our careers, have children, and raise them. From the pinnacle of our self-made world we will then watch our children do the same. They will grow up, date, find work, marry, advance in their careers, and have their children.

We learn this formula for happiness from the people around us and from books, movies, newspapers, and magazines. Society teaches us these activities are satisfying and "right" in themselves.

But without intimacy, any activity eventually palls, grows empty.

Whether we have chosen a traditional or nontraditional lifestyle, without intimacy most of us will begin to realize some important quality is missing from our lives. "Is this all there is?" we wonder.

And so we divorce. Or we grow angry and disillusioned. Or we have bouts of loneliness and depression. Sometimes we turn to drink and pills to fill the aching void within us. Or we simply grow distant, cold, and cut off from everyone, as my friend Jerry did.

But with the presence of intimacy, the fairy-tale ideal of "and they lived happily ever after" can take on some realistic meanings.

With intimacy, we can weather life's storms armed with unflinching love.

With intimacy, we can dare to look within at our own terrifying demons and know we are still loved.

With intimacy, we can choose from the feast of life's offerings what is best and most appropriate for us.

Together, lovingly, you and I in the pages of this book can explore our built-in capacity for intimacy. Together we can begin to learn how to create the special intimacies that are most satisfying to each of us, because you and I—together—have a chance to grow more happily, fully human.

CHAPTER 2

BEING FULLY HUMAN

> In the child, consciousness rises out of the depths of unconscious psychic life, at first like separate islands, which gradually unite to form a "continent," a continuous landmass of consciousness. Progressive mental development means, in effect, extension of consciousness. With the rise of a continuous consciousness, and not before, psychological relationship becomes possible.
>
> —C.G. JUNG
> *Marriage as a Psychological Relationship*

intimate adj (1) a: intrinsic, essential; b: belonging to or characterizing one's deepest nature (2) marked by very close association, contact, or familiarity (3) a: marked by a warm friendship developing through long association; b: suggesting informal warmth or privacy (4) of a very personal or private nature.

—WEBSTER'S NINTH NEW COLLEGIATE DICTIONARY

Intimacy, the state of being intimate.

Intimacy is what I need in my life.

Intimacy is what you need in your life.

And we're not talking about simple "familiarity," but instead about what Webster's refers to as "belonging to or characterizing one's deepest nature."

Intimacy is intensely subjective, and there are as many definitions as there are people's individual needs.

All of us come from different backgrounds. Even in the same family, the third child's experience is not going to be the same as the first's. Each of us has different hopes, different deficiencies, different strengths, different concepts of what our rights as human beings are. Just as the young woman in the previous chapter struggled to explain why she was lonely even though surrounded by people, we struggle to define what is missing or needs to be changed in our lives.

Because of this, intimacy can appear to be an amorphous, ill-defined concept.

But the very human qualities that divide us also unite us.

Whether we aspire to be a bank president or a teacher, all of us share the act of aspiring. Whether we are more frightened by the spiders in our room or by the potential of nuclear holocaust, all of us have fears. Whether we enjoy walks on the seashore or games of chess, each of us has the ability to enjoy.

In the large picture, we humans share certain universal elements, and on the basis of these I have evolved the following definition:

Intimacy is the transcendent self expressing and fulfilling itself in relationship with another.

Transcendent—an experience that lifts us above the mundane in life. Intimacy goes beyond the ordinary. It is not simply a handshake in the hall or a weekly bridge game.

Intimacy is primarily a spiritual experience.

But it is also an emotional experience.

And it is a physical experience, maybe.

Knock out the spiritual and you do not have intimacy. Put in the physical and you do not necessarily have intimacy.

The transcendent experience of intimacy raises the human to new levels of love, both for another and for oneself. I use the term 'spiritual' as a synonym for transcendence. I am not giving any specific religious, denominational, or cultish association whatever to the word.

Without intimacy we cannot have the ultimate experience of affirmation, and we all need affirmation very, very much.

Only when we drop the half-truths and lies that we use as shields to "protect" ourselves can we know—really know—that we are loved. When our intimate self goes unseen and unshared, the negative parts of us tend to inflate into out-of-control monsters. But when we let another person know us honestly, then the fearful child or awful demon that dwells within each of us can transform from temper tantrums and loneliness into warm confidence, self-esteem, and love.

And when another person allows us the privilege of intimacy, we see a reflection of our own humanness and the miracle of life. That in itself is affirmation, and a major step toward becoming fully human.

"All my life, I've been independent, never really needed anyone," the man in my office told me. He was an athlete in his early thirties, peaking at his career, and exploring a significant new relationship. "I've been very successful because of it, or so I thought. Now here I am, giving up my independence, my freedom, but I feel stronger than ever. It's so different, I can't explain it. What's happening to me?"

Spiritually and emotionally, intimacy is an opening, a sharing of autonomy. It is also a giving up and giving away of what we sometimes mistakenly refer to as autonomy.

Real autonomy is important. It means each of us taking full responsibility for our own lives, for evolving into the best human beings we can evolve into, occupying our own space. And that also means not brooking any interference from others who through fear or stupidity would stop us. In autonomy, we are the fulfillers of our own life scripts, and the exercisers of our own physical, emotional, and spiritual energies.

I've spent a lot of my lifetime helping people, including myself, to achieve a measure of autonomy, and the experience of autonomy is absolutely magnificent.

But as with many other wonderful things we can experience, autonomy can be abused. Unfortunately, what sometimes passes for autonomy is unbridled, unmitigated selfishness. In its extreme form, it can sound like this: To hell with the rest of the world—I'm going to get what I want when I want it because I'm entitled to do what I please.

That isn't true. No one is entitled to get what they want when they want it from anyone. That is not autonomy. That is selfishness and greed. That is destruction and even death.

Real autonomy is life. Real autonomy is openness.

Intimacy is the sharing of real autonomy.

Autonomy does not have to be kept only to oneself. In fact, autonomy grows in strength when it's shared. In the beginning of a good relationship, as we grow accustomed to new ways of relating, the sharing is delightful but sometimes bumpy. It can sound like this:

> It's me in my emergent wholeness, learning to fly like a butterfly coming out of a chrysalis, who wants to share this journey through life with you. We are both responsible for our own flights. We've both experienced what it's like to be caterpillars doomed to crawling to get where we wanted to go. Now we've come out of the darkness of our cocoons, through the long dark nights of our souls, and into the light.
>
> You and I together can share the wonderful discoveries of life, but to do that, I must expose myself. I must be vulnerable to you, take risks the kind of which I'm rarely called upon to take. I must risk your knowing who I *really* am.
>
> Yes, you and I will fly together, two separate beings whose togetherness creates an even greater autonomy—an autonomy for our relationship. We share our mutual independence and become interdependent. We fly with strength, courage, and love because we have ourselves, each other, and our growing intimacy.

* * *

There are many kinds of intimacies. Some are momentary, yet so important they affect us for life. Others are long-term relationships that become the centers of our existence. And in between spreads an array of limitless opportunities for human transformation through intimacy.

As Willa Cather wrote in *Shadows on the Rock,* "Sometimes a neighbor whom we have disliked a lifetime for his arrogance and conceit lets fall a single commonplace remark that shows us another side, another man, really; a man uncertain, and puzzled, and in the dark like ourselves." This was a fleeting intimacy, but treasured like a rose pressed between the pages of a book.

Another example is the intimacy between parents and child. Children who learn the meaning of intimacy from their parents have scripts of love that will last throughout their lives. Very, very lucky indeed are such children.

An intimate child-parent relationship includes appropriate physical expression as well as the emotional and spiritual qualities we've discussed. How can you be intimate with your child without holding him, without hugging her, without kissing him or her, without allowing the child to feel the wonderful appropriate fusion of bodies as the child is rocked and loved?

Some of us try to recapture that incredible feeling for the rest of our lives—the total physical, emotional, and spiritual security that exists when our primary needs for food and warmth are being met by the loving parent in a safe environment.

Those of us who are parents must ask ourselves frequently: Does our child know and experience our love?

And this doesn't mean just when they're little. Does your fifteen-year-old boy know he's loved in the sense of the intimacy we've been talking about? Does your seventeen-year-old girl know she is loved? Then it gets a little more difficult as the years go by. What about your twenty-eight-year-old daughter, your forty-five-year-old son? Do they know they are loved, really loved? Can you show them openness, vulnerability, intimacy?

What about your parents? Sometimes sharing appropriate intimacy with parents is even more difficult than it is with children. But our parents gave us life, brought us into the world, loved us to the best of their abilities. And they were the object of our first intimate love.

Can you tell your parents you love them? Can you be intimate with your parents?

And of course we have myriad other opportunities for intimacy—brothers, sisters, other relatives, lovers, friends, neighbors, coworkers, clerks in stores. We are indeed surrounded by people, and we don't have to feel lonely.

Intimacy isn't always easy, but it's not impossible to achieve either.

I talked with a group of businessmen last year who believed they had real, intimate relationships with their employees. Their intentions were good, but they were mistaken. No one can have a truly intimate relationship with an employee (or an employer) because the two are unequal, and equality is essential for intimacy.

If you can hire and fire, move employees around and transfer them, change their whole lives by the power of your authority, you cannot have an intimate relationship. We take out insurance against intimacy by calling all kinds of other relationships intimate, when they cannot possibly contain the transformational qualities inherent in true intimacy.

* * *

"I've never felt anything like it," the middle-aged woman in my office told me. Her eyes were bright, her skin was glowing. Following a bitter divorce and ten years alone, she had recently married for a second time. "I've heard about it, read about it, but I never thought it could happen for me!"

In the sacrament of sexual intimacy, two adults unite in a transcendent moment of time.

Through the emotional, spiritual, and physical intimacy of loving sex, each person is lifted beyond the self. Two people join in perhaps the ultimate expression of being truly human.

Any person can have a sexual relationship with another person without intimacy.

How I wish every single child born on this Earth were the product of intimacy in the sense I've been using it. Unhappily, this is far from the case.

Instead too many children are born from the same environment in which too many adults spend their lives—surviving, not living, never experiencing the transcendental opportunities of intimacy.

Intimacy is like a tree, with deep roots and a wide, spreading canopy of leafy branches. It is a tree of life.

People with no intimacy in their lives lead starved existences with shallow roots and spindly branches on which few leaves will grow.

Partial intimacies are often vital to our lives. My intimate relationship with my dying friend Jerry was one of these. It was precious and unforgettable, and I will forever be influenced by it. But the intimate relationship was incomplete, a branch on my tree of life.

I think the intimate relationship between a man and a woman with a total commitment represents the peak of the fruit that our tree is capable of growing.

Some trees grow other fruit. Other experiences of intimacy produce different fruit and very beautiful trees.

But for the purposes of this book, we will discuss primarily how to achieve happy, loving, lasting intimate relationships between adults willing to take the enormous risk of complete commitment.

And as old-fashioned as that commitment may seem, it goes like this:

> I, John, take thee Mary to be my lawful wedded wife, to have and to hold from this day forward, for better, for worse, for richer, for poorer, in sickness and in health, until death us do part.

The wedding ceremony may not be as important as the commitment, but in our society, our culture, the universal symbol for commitment is marriage.

It's not surprising that even though a couple has lived together for years, when they at last decide to marry, their relationship changes, sometimes deteriorates, even ending in divorce within a few months.

Why? Because living together is not necessarily a commitment. And the act of marrying forces us, often unconsciously, to face our willingness—or unwillingness—to make a commitment.

Living together can be another insurance policy against intimacy. We hide the lack of commitment behind proximity. "I'm here every night, sleeping in the same bed. Isn't that enough?"

No one can answer that question except yourself. Is it enough? Many people say they go through life quite happily without a committed intimate relationship. Perhaps they do.

But in my experience, the human being without committed intimacy yearns for its transcendental experience. It's natural, our right, and the destiny of being fully human.

* * *

Once a farmer saw a hunter shoot and kill an eagle. The farmer knew there was a baby eaglet in the nest, only a few days old, and it would die without its mother. So the farmer climbed up to the nest and rescued it. He took it to his farm, tried all sorts of ways to nurture it, but the eaglet wouldn't respond.

At last, in desperation, he put it in the barnyard in the nest of a mother hen who had just hatched a lot of eggs. The hen included the eaglet with her chicks and raised it to be a chicken.

The eaglet thought it was a chicken, too, and when it grew old enough to fly, the farmer had a difficult job convincing the bird it was indeed an eagle. But at last he did, and the young, proud eagle soared away on steady wings into his own, natural destiny.

You and I are capable of applying the appropriate kinds of intimacy we need to every kind of human relationship that exists.

Like the eagle, in intimacy we learn to fly. So be intimate. Be an eagle and learn to fly. Give and receive in all of your relationships, but especially create a fulfilling, committed love relationship, for it will give a center to your life.

Learn to fly in the mountains of intimacy, your natural habitat, rather than to be locked forever into the barnyard of mere relationship.

CHAPTER 3

THE FEAR OF INTIMACY

So far as we know, consciousness is always ego-consciousness. In order to be conscious of myself, I must be able to distinguish myself from others. Relationship can only take place where this distinction exists.

—C.G. JUNG
Marriage as a Psychological Relationship

"I get really scared if I start to feel good," one of my clients said recently to me. "My anxiety rises so rapidly that I begin to sabotage what I want most, which is just that—feeling good."

Why is it so difficult for us to experience emotional fulfillment? When we do begin to feel happy, why do we run away, deliberately sabotage the experience, or let the opportunity for happiness pass us by?

Physically it's as if we were starving, but we throw sand on the meal that was prepared to meet our need for food. It's as if we were lost in the middle of a desert, dying of thirst, but we pour poison into the water of the only oasis.

Sometimes we treat intimacy like that. We throw something obnoxious into the relationship. We poison it. We make impossible the fulfillment of what intimacy is meant to fulfill.

Sadly, we sabotage the presence of what emotionally and spiritually we need.

There are many very complicated reasons for this, and although we can't address all of them here, two are particularly significant because they are frequent and powerful. You might recognize them in yourself or in others. They are:

- Fear of Success
- Fear of Abandonment

One of the foremost reasons we unconsciously destroy our intimate relationships is our fear of success.

Once thought to be simply the fear of failure, we now understand that fear of success is a separate and distinctly real motivator for many of us. With this fear, we cannot allow ourselves to get too successful because success makes us emotionally uncomfortable, even frightens us. For those with this affliction, a great triumph can be as terrifying as an abysmal failure is for others.

Many of us are caught in the terrible prison between both fears. We learn quickly to stay within our rigid comfort zone, never venturing too close to either success or to failure. With the pain of the two fears we build our own prison. We forget that since we built the prison, we also can tear down its walls and free ourselves.

To a person afraid of success, intimacy is especially menacing. There is a lot of work involved in achieving intimacy, which means you cannot sneak up on the success and fool yourself with your stealth. You must actively participate in creating successful intimacy, and your fear of success is going to be constantly triggered.

And then there's the additional trauma of a major life-style change. The changes can be as picky as which way to hang the toilet paper roll, or as painful as whose name goes on which bank accounts. The changes can cause frustration, resentment, and anger as each of you adjusts to new living conditions. No one can introduce a new relationship that meets such a primary need as intimacy into an existing life-style without adjusting the life-style. And your changes will be radical if it is the first real intimate relationship you've ever had. In fact, our discovery of the intimacy we believe to be within our grasp is often triggered by the pain of the way we are living. When the pain of loneliness or disillusionment grows so great that we need an alternative, most of us discover the alternative is intimacy.

Settling disputes through communication is fertile ground for the relationship's death or growth and is often a reflection of our fear of success. If we refuse to face the disputes, the relationship can become gravely ill, even die. On the other hand, if we try to resolve disagreements, all of our alarms sound because our fear of success is assaulted.

Sometimes we have an unspoken agreement to resolve the little disputes but to ignore the big, volatile ones. This gives a facade of peace and success that is without foundation. Often the greater the apparent success of a relationship, the closer to failure it really is.

But, on the other hand, if we face our disagreements, talk about them, and resolve them, our relationship can grow stronger, rooted in a mutual respect that honors the unique needs of each person and of the relationship itself.

* * *

You begin a relationship. It looks and feels very good. Everything about it seems green for go. You begin to feel as if you've never had it so good. There's tremendous compatibility. *Did you realize that what you just said was what I was going to say? This is uncanny!* You touch hands while you're standing on a nylon carpet. The air is dry. Bzzzz! *Did you feel that electric current go off between us? I've never felt that before. I even dreamt about you last night.*

Don't ever trust a relationship about which you dream a lot for the simple reason that if the relationship were healthy, in the economy of dreaming, you would tend not to dream about it. You tend to dream only about people or events that are disturbing you. Your daytime consciousness can handle the goodies, the delicious M&Ms of life.

What we do not handle in terms of consciousness we flush down the toilet of the night and it regurgitates in the form of dreams. And so when you say to someone, "You are the man (or woman) of my dreams," remember what you're probably dreaming about is the male or the female counterpart of what you cannot deal with in your own psyche.

But say you have begun a very exciting relationship. It's wonderful, and you see limitless reasons why it should work. At last you're beginning to experience true intimacy and it's making you happy beyond your wildest expectations.

Then a familiar pattern begins to emerge—you're testing the

new person in your life, testing to see how much you are loved. This happens frequently to both men and women, no matter how much they love, or are loved by, the other person in their life.

A few years ago a friend of mine whom I'll call Charlie found himself caught in this kind of situation. He had become resigned to the likelihood that he would never have anything except superficial relationships because the women he loved eventually didn't pass his tests or they would leave him.

Then he fell in love with Kate. He was beside himself with joy and excitement. She was perfect for him, the most lovely woman he'd ever met, both physically and emotionally. They were incredibly compatible. They enjoyed many activities together, yet respected each other's different interests. They laughed, talked, played together. When he wasn't with her, his thoughts would return to her often. And when he was with her, he had a sense of love he'd only read about. They married.

Then Charlie began to feel the fine edge of jealousy, an emotion honed by an earlier, failed marriage. As the jealousy grew more intense, it began to masquerade as a possessive love. We often unconsciously choose possessive love over jealousy because possessive love seems less offensive, less primitive.

He told Kate, "Because I love you so much I want to know everything about you."

Then he asked her questions. Did you go to that restaurant before? Who were you with? What did you do? Or—Have you seen that movie? Who did you go with? What did you do afterwards? Did you sleep with him?

Patiently she answered his questions and reassured him, but nothing seemed to satisfy him. He increased the insidious game's ante, asking more difficult questions, testing her truthfulness because eventually he might catch her saying something incorrect about her past. This is an extremely subtle form of hostility.

She was surprised by his behavior, then confused.

"Have you ever been to La Jolla?" he asked her. She told him no. Maybe she had forgotten, or maybe she was simply exhausted from his endless questions. Then a few weeks later he discovered she had indeed been to La Jolla.

"Why didn't you tell me?" he demanded.

Now she was angry, really angry. "Because I'm sick and tired of the way you keep digging into my past! None of that matters. I'm here with you now. I love you now!" So they agreed not to talk about it again. But by then he was courting trouble. If she had lied to him about La Jolla, she could be lying about her love for him and, even more important to his fears, she could be lying that she would never abandon him.

Not dealing with this situation could have destroyed their marriage. And with Charlie's history of intimacy problems, that probably would have made it impossible for him to ever have had an intimate relationship again.

But Charlie fortunately could not keep the agreement with Kate. His unconscious fears refused to be denied. Again he delved into her past, trying to catch her in lies.

She insisted they get counseling. Faced with the loss of intimacy, Charlie—who knew too well life without intimacy—summoned his courage and went to counseling.

In therapy, Charlie learned about his fear of abandonment, which was directly attached to a childhood fear each of us has.

For men, the fear is of losing their mothers. For women, the fear is of losing their fathers. When we grow to be adults, the continuation of this fear indicates a shaky self-esteem, another common problem. Once Kate understood, she forgave Charlie and saw the importance of her own symbolic role in his fears.

Kate learned to deal with Charlie's questions by reaching out to him. She held his hand, refused to answer, but instead told him she loved him very much. Charlie learned to discipline himself, to pay attention to what he was saying and doing when he fed his testing disease, and to focus on the love he shared with Kate.

In this way they starved to death Charlie's questioning, which was destructive to her, to him, and to their relationship.

Although they experienced times when his testing again got out of control and when she would lose her temper with exasperation, gradually having her tell him that she loved him became more pleasurable to him than his miserable questioning had been.

At last he gave up the investigation of her past. Once he did that, their relationship again reached new heights of intimacy and love. For the first time they could share their personal histories with safety.

They had faced a terrible problem together, one that had threatened their future, and they had succeeded in solving it.

Just as all of us do, they will continue to have problems in life, some minor, others that will shake again the foundation of their relationship. But now they have something only experience can give—knowledge they can work together, they can trust and rely on each other. Their love is real and vitally important to both of them.

*   *   *

Testing doesn't have to be just asking questions about the past. It can take other forms. Think about your present intimate relationship, or perhaps do a little autopsy on one that has failed, and see whether any of these sound familiar:

"Because I want our home to be the place for our perfect love, our home should be perfect, too. Why are all these fingerprints by the door?"

"I love you so much that I'm going to buy you all this beautiful underwear to inspire you to lose weight. Then you'll be the same girl I married."

"I want sex with you twice a day only because I love you so much."

"Even though my first wife was a better cook than you, I love you much more."

"Even though my first husband could fix things around the house, I love you much more."

"Since you really love me, let's extend our love, share it more with other people. We'll invite my parents over every weekend for dinner."

All roads of testing in a relationship lead to abandonment. Part of the test is to see how far you can push the other person. The object is to have the person fail the test, and the subtlety is that you're trying to give the impression you want the person to pass it. Eventually the testing will drive the wonderful person in your life away: "Enough, I'm leaving," he says.

"I always knew you'd abandon me," she says.

* * *

When intimacy is something we long for, why would we sabotage our most important relationship?

When we think about intimacy and how fundamental it is to our lives, and when we realize how often we destroy its success, we easily can conclude that something profound has to be happening in the saboteur. In most cases, I believe the person is caught in the terror of abandonment, closely followed by a similar fear, that of rejection.

This is how it works:

> The more intimate I get with you, the more vulnerable I become. The more you get to know me, the more I am likely to lose you because to know me is *not* to love me.
>
> If you know me less well, you might love me more.
>
> If you know me too intimately, you will realize how inadequate I am, how fearful I am, how insecure I am, how worthless I am, how unlovable I am, how lonely I am, and what a loser I feel that I really am. I am not worthy to be loved by anybody, especially someone as marvelous as you.

When your fears of abandonment and rejection are great enough, you begin to hedge your intimacy bets. You take out insurance against loss. Testing is a favorite form of insurance.

This is how testing works:

> Before I commit myself to a totally intimate relationship with you, which means taking the gigantic risk with all its deep

psychic undertones that you may abandon me, I'm going to test you.

I'm going to see whether the way you feel about me is really the way you say you feel about me. And I can test you in all kinds of ways.

I can play a kind of Russian roulette game with you. And each time you pass one question, one test, by staying with me, that just shows me how vulnerable I really am, and so I will increase the ante the next time. I will make it harder and harder for you, and I will keep on and on and on until you eventually fail a test or leave me. And then I can say: Ha! I knew it all along!

It doesn't matter what I've been doing, whether I've been unfaithful, whether I've kept other bargains in our relationship, I knew eventually you would abandon me.

Thank God I didn't commit myself.

There are many ways to sabotage intimacy, and all of them seem to relate to the simple proposition that if we don't enter the race, if we don't commit ourselves, then we can't lose.

If we withhold our commitment until we've finished testing, we will almost certainly test our intimate relationships beyond their endurance to survive. That way we never have to make a commitment, and we will simply prove the unconscious contention we've held all along that we're not capable of being loved, and that we will always—inevitably!—be abandoned.

Recognizing that you or your partner is a "tester" is the first step toward facing and resolving this potential destroyer of intimate relationships. Many people have successfully resolved the problem, and you can, too.

* * *

Most of us caught in the grip of the unconscious fear of abandonment see only the results—that our relationships fail.

But once we begin to understand how the fear of abandonment works, and that unknowingly we sabotage our relationships, we have moved into productive new territory.

Now the fear is conscious. Now we have some idea of what we or our partner has been doing.

All we need is an inkling to begin to see our own roles—are we testers, victims, or among the noninvolved? We can listen to the way we talk, pay attention to the words we use, see our sabotaging behavior. When we understand what unconsciously we have been doing, we can begin to change. We can rewrite the automatic scripts that have been running our lives. We can break free into new ways of living that are appropriate for us, that will make us happy.

In this conscious stage, the fear of abandonment becomes a challenge. We can face this challenge as we face others—by making a commitment, taking risks. If we do, something wonderful begins to happen:

> I reach out, risking rejection. I realize that the more risks I take to make this wonderful transcendent relationship work, the more I placate my fears. By expressing the gift of intimacy, I find I can make my own happiness.

Later in this book we will do an in-depth exploration of commitment and the ways you can make your intimate relationship work, but for now let's assume you have already reached this stage in your intimacy development. You have discovered that committed intimacy means freedom. You no longer fear your partner will abandon you. You no longer fear you will abandon your partner. You have built an increasingly fulfilling life together. You are successful, happy in your love.

Then a suffocating cloak of darkness falls on you. There is one more fear left—or at least it seems like a fear, and it feels like the biggest fear of abandonment there is. Death.

I remember the first time I faced this "fear" myself. It was on a warm, sunny day when my wife Ingrid and I were outside gardening. We were working side by side, planting a fruit tree, talking, thoroughly enjoying each other. Suddenly Ingrid sat down.

I turned, reached for her.

She was in obvious discomfort. Her hands were pressed

against her chest. Haltingly she told me she had been short of breath lately.

She recovered quickly, and we saw our doctor who found she had a minor respiratory problem that medication easily remedied. We were lucky.

But in that one moment when I looked into Ingrid's eyes and saw her physical pain I saw our future, too. My mind said, "Oh, my God! This can't be. What would happen if she were to have a heart attack? Die? How could I deal with it?"

On the way to the doctor, I went silently through these thoughts: "I'm six years older than Ingrid, and statistically women live longer than men. So I'm going to die twelve, thirteen, maybe fourteen years before she does." That made me feel better. Then I saw the consequences—I was wishing my death on her so she would have to deal with a problem I didn't want to face.

In effect, I hoped to abandon her before she abandoned me.

As we have seen, in the first abandonment stage in relationships, we act out of unconscious fear, the child terrified of losing the parent. In the second stage, we act out of the conscious fear of commitment. With both of these fears, conscious or unconscious choice triggers abandonment. We are acting out of fear.

But death is not an abandonment. Death is part of life, part of wholeness. The greatest honor we can pay someone we love intimately is to let them go when their life with us needs to end. As Carl Jung points out, birth and death make a single curve, and life ends in the state of repose from which it began.

When my wife needs to let go of this physical life, or when I need to let go, death is not abandonment. If I in my ego-filled dependency won't let her go even though her body is full of pain and suffering, that's not loving. Is she abandoning me because her body is crying for release? Not at all.

Instead, allowing our partner to die with love and peace is part of the continuing gift we give the other to be who each is.

Unlike abandonment, natural death is not an arbitrary choice. It is not a manipulation of one partner by the other. It is not a retreat from intimacy. Again as Dr. Jung says: paradoxically, death is the goal of life.

When you hold your partner, or your partner holds you, as we take our leave from this life, our mutual love is being expressed through this most profound sharing.

And so, I hope that each of you reaches the stage in your intimate relationship when you confront this ultimate issue. Recognizing its significance, and that death is not the supreme abandonment, will help you to move beyond fear and into the unfolding joys of living intimacy.

CHAPTER 4

REWARDS OR COSTS?

> . . . although the distinction [between oneself and others] may be made in a general way, normally it is incomplete, because large areas of psychic life still remain unconscious.
>
> As no distinction can be made with regard to unconscious contents, on this terrain no relationship can be established; here there still reigns the original unconscious condition of the ego's primitive identity with others, in other words a complete absence of relationship.
>
> —C.G. JUNG
> *Marriage as a Psychological Relationship*

We are accustomed to working. It's part of our daily lives. Not long ago I saw a bumper sticker that said: "I owe, I owe. So off to work I go." We work to earn money, to earn recognition, to make a place for ourselves in this world.

We also work, we hope, because we get satisfaction from learning, from doing something well, and from the acceptance and recognition of our peers. Whether we are barbers, lawyers, or accountants, whether we raise horses, keep house, manage money, fly jets, or collect stamps, we are a people who like to work.

So we get to the issue of working to create and sustain intimacy.

We talk about wanting intimacy, craving intimacy, willing to do anything for just one experience of total intimacy.

Then we talk about the responsibilities of intimacy, the commitment of intimacy, the work of intimacy, and, suddenly, we start to back off. Many promising intimate relationships fail because one or both of those involved don't want to do the work.

In a sense, it's understandable. There are very obvious rewards involved with other kinds of work.

Oftentimes we're known by our jobs. He's the doctor down the street. She's the real estate agent on the corner. He teaches history at the high school. She's the new rabbi. He's a plumber, and a darn good one, too.

Seldom are we known for our intimacy work.

The rewards of intimacy are not public. They are very, very private. The biggest recognition of the work of intimacy comes from within one's own self and from the other person in the relationship. That's it. No salary, no job title, no guarantees for advancement, not even a company car or a pension.

The work of intimacy is perhaps the greatest risk in the world. It triggers in us fears of success, abandonment, and rejection. What if we go to all that work and the relationship fails? Does that mean we're a failure, that we're incapable of intimacy?

Absolutely not. It means simply that the relationship didn't work out. That's all. There is no "good" or "bad" attached to you or to the other person in a failed relationship.

But there is a bonus.

You can learn from a failed relationship, particularly a failed relationship at which you've worked. That's one of the ways you discover who you are—by choosing what you like and dislike, what you're comfortable with, what you enjoy doing most.

By making choices you strengthen your self-knowledge, and if your choices don't coincide comfortably with the person with whom you'd hoped to have a long-lasting, committed, intimate relationship, then how wonderful that you are leaving the relationship with at least the richness of those discoveries.

If you had not worked at the relationship, you would have learned little about yourself, and the relationship would have failed anyway.

By increasing your self-knowledge, you also increase your chances of finding the right person for the lasting intimate relationship in which you will reap the most happiness.

* * *

At one point in the Broadway musical, *Hello, Dolly!* Dolly suggests to a lonely but resistent rich man that he snuggle up to his cash register because at least it rings. That situation has never appealed to me, and I doubt that it will appeal to you. So let's get to this demanding but exciting work of intimacy. We'll begin by examining some of the relationship qualities involved.

Draw a chart like the one below on a piece of paper, or imagine one in your mind:

REWARD	COST

My job will be to pose a series of words for you to consider. Each represents a quality inherent in intimate relationships. Your job will be to think about each word and then to enter it on your chart.

As we talk about the qualities individually, consider whether it is a reward or a cost to you in your relationship. Listen to your inner voices. Although the words are simple, they are difficult to measure honestly. They are the stuff of intimacy.

You can gloss over them and say, "Yes—reward, reward, reward. If I'm having problems in my relationship, or I don't have an intimate relationship, it isn't because of those words."

In a sense, you're right. It's the meaning of the words that makes your part in a relationship work or not work. And that's why these words are important. They signify some of the characteristics of intimacy. And they are very difficult to measure honestly, especially when applied to an ongoing intimate relationship.

All of us, including me, struggle with intimacy and becoming vulnerable. I can't always answer reward to each of the words I pose. But until I identify the ones that make me uneasy, the ones that seem more of a cost than a benefit, I am powerless to change my attitudes and behaviors. I must know myself in order to grow the transcendent experience of intimacy with another.

If you don't have a significant relationship now, you can apply this test to a relationship in your past. Or if you don't have that, or prefer not to think about past relationships because they are absolutely unthinkable, you can apply the qualities to what you intend to have in a future intimate relationship. Remember, self-honesty is a sword against unhappiness.

* * *

TIME

How much time do you spend with the person in your major intimate relationship?

Absentmindedly you kiss good-bye in the morning as one or both of you go off to work (or maybe on a particularly hectic day you don't have time to kiss at all). Exhausted, you meet again after five o'clock. One of you goes into the kitchen to cook, the other collapses with the newspaper. The kids demand your attention. The telephone rings. Someone turns on the television. You eat dinner in a distracted haze. Afterwards, someone has to wash the dishes and tidy the kitchen. Someone needs to spend time with the kids, bathe and read to them perhaps, or help them with their homework. If you have no children, then there is the laundry to do, the bills to pay, friends to call, the house and cars to maintain, maybe work from the office to complete, hobbies to pursue.

Does any of this sound like your situation? In the past few years, researchers have been increasingly studying intimacy in marriage and significant relationships. In one study, couples were asked how much time they spent in intimate conversation with one another. All the couples had been married or living together four or five years. The average of their answers was twenty-three minutes a day.

That's it—twenty-three minutes out of a possible twenty-four hours a day with the person each considered most important to his or her life.

It's astounding to realize you and the person closest to you probably spend less time together now than you did two or three years ago, but more time than you will in another two or three years. Not very encouraging, is it?

And then there's eye contact. The ancient Greeks considered our eyes to be windows to our souls. Researchers have discovered something not very surprising—when a couple first meet they look often and lovingly into one another's eyes. But after that, eye contact is all downhill. After four or five years of marriage or living together, they seldom look at one other at all.

So if in a typical relationship we hardly take the time to talk with or look at one another, how can we be intimate?

There are many demands on our time. We must work to earn livings. We have certain obligations to fulfill to others. We must perform certain essential tasks just to get from day to day.

But after we've taken care of all those obligations, don't you think there are more than twenty-three minutes a day we can spend talking meaningfully with the person we love most?

How would you feel if your intimate other—your wife, your husband, or your lover—said to you:

"Hey, did you realize that now that we're married (or living together) we can spend all kinds of wonderful time together?"

"Have you noticed how few meals we eat together?"

"Have you noticed how little actual unbroken time in our priority of relationships we give to each other?"

"Have you noticed how little we value this relationship compared with all the other demands on our time?"

"I would really like us to change our priorities."

"I want to spend as much time with you as possible, beginning right now."

How does that make you feel—happy or unhappy? excited or panicked? Is time with your partner a reward or a cost?

COMMUNICATING LOVE

Sometimes relationships seem superficially amusing in the way one partner avoids telling the other *I love you.*

> HIM: Do you love me?
> HER: Do I love you? For twenty years I've cleaned the house, raised the kids, given your dinner parties, washed your clothes. After all these years, why ask?
> HIM: But do you love me?
> HER: For twenty years I've lived with you, argued with you, worried with you, worried *about* you, slept with you! What do you think love is?
> HIM: Then you do love me?

A man I knew once said to me, "Of course I love her. I don't get drunk, and I don't beat her up. My God, of course I love her."

Well, with those kinds of criteria for intimacy, I must love every woman in the world because I don't beat any up and I don't get drunk!

How can you be intimate without saying *I love you*?

It is important to show your love for the other person, but it is equally important to say it. And it is important for you to hear it from this person whom you love so much. Tevye, that endearing patriarch from *Fiddler on the Roof,* like most of us, didn't want to know how many times his wife had darned his socks as much as he wanted her to tell him simply, honestly, straightforwardly the truth—did she or did she not love him?

I love you—the three most beautiful words in our language. They cost nothing to say but, when they're true, they are priceless, and with them you can buy the world.

How easy is it for you to say *I love you*? If it's easy, then you've discovered that not saying the words is hard. The phrase tends to bubble out often, spontaneously, happily.

Do you find saying the words embarrassing? Are you embarrassed to hear your partner say them to you? Does the phrase put you on the spot? Does it compel you to think, "Oh, my God, what am I supposed to say now?" Or, "What does she (or he) want from me?"

Is hearing *I love you* a reward or a cost?

Is saying *I love you* a reward or a cost?

ENERGY

Compared with the energy you put into the development of your career, business, family commitments, social life, or any other compartment in your life, how much of your energy goes into the development of your intimate relationship?

In some intimacies, both partners feel as if they receive a wealth of energy and attention. Together they create a feast of life. The relationship seems to generate its own energy, yet that is only because it is constantly fueled by both partners. As one client told me, "The energy that I get from the meeting of my need for intimacy has galvanized my life." In this case, the measure of energy is obviously beneficial, a reward.

Or do you find yourself not giving much energy or attention to your intimate relationship? Does it seem to you that your partner is constantly, unrealistically demanding energy from you that you don't have, ignoring all the other calls upon you from the other departments of your life? If you feel this way, the cost factor has become paramount.

Energy—is it a reward for you, or a cost?

MONEY

Do you ever stop to think: How much is this relationship costing me? If so, you have a lot of company. Money is one criterion set by society for judging the success or failure of anything, including relationships. If your relationship is draining you financially dry, you probably cannot afford it. If however your relationship is meeting your intimacy needs, which are beyond price, then the rewards are priceless, beyond cost.

Money—reward or cost?

LAUGHTER

Laughter seems easy, but it's just as difficult as the other tests. Many, many people live together and never laugh. And if somebody does laugh, the other one says, "Hey, what do you think you're laughing at?" But intimacy needs humor and fun, needs the ability to laugh with each other without ever being made to feel vulnerable to attack.

Laughing with your partner is very rewarding. But being laughed at extracts a heavy price in self-esteem and worth.

In your relationship, laughter—is it a reward or a cost?

CRYING

"For God's sake, what's the matter with you now? Don't I have enough problems without you whining and yelping like a scalded cat?"

"How wonderful it is that you can share your tears with me."

"I'm sorry you're crying, but I'm glad you're crying with me." Crying with someone brings the reward of empathy. But crying *because* of someone is a price no relationship can afford too often. Crying—reward or cost?

SILLINESS

Very close to laughter, but not quite the same, is silliness. Sharing the childlike (not childish—and there is a difference) ability to be silly shows a person's feeling of tremendous security in a relationship. Silliness adds elements of joy, abandon, and whimsy, all refreshing qualities that help to keep an intimate relationship forever fresh and alive.

Silliness—reward or cost?

GIVING AND RECEIVING

You cannot have intimacy without giving, and by giving I'm not referring simply to birthday and anniversary gifts, although those sorts of thoughtful surprises (not bought by your secretary, please) often bring delight.

The very basic condition of intimacy requires sharing and togetherness, and giving is fundamental to both. But this kind of giving is from deep inside, from the secrets of your life. It is also the act of stepping back so your partner can do something he or she wants.

Sometimes the most difficult aspect of giving is the other side of it—receiving, accepting. Some of us can give, but we find accepting the same sort of kindness and consideration in return difficult. Others find receiving easy, but are baffled by giving.

Giving—reward or cost?

Receiving—reward or cost?

CARING

Caring for another person often shows in the little acts of human kindness that fill our days with the quiet, secure feeling of being wanted. Do you think about your partner, what his or her life away from you is like? When you really care, you're interested. You ask questions designed not to probe, but to encourage conversation. You listen thoughtfully, not to be "good," but because you really want to know. You notice your partner's likes and dislikes. You notice when your partner shows care for you. You care that you are cared for.

If caring takes too much time, too much effort, and seems a rewardless occupation, then it is a cost for you in your relationship.

Caring—reward or cost?

TOUCHING

A warm hug, a tender squeeze of the hand, a tear wiped from a cheek—these are acts of intimacy. How can anyone be intimate without touching?

Touching—reward or cost?

SILENCE

Do the silences in your home drive you to distraction? They will if they are filled with hostility and punishing withdrawal. But if your mutual silences are companionable times of reflection, they can occur only in a nurturing environment, and silence is a golden reward in your intimate relationship.

Silence—reward or cost?

LANGUAGE

Language can be a rapier to slash and maim, or it can be the instrument by which you communicate your innermost thoughts to the one whom you love most in the world.

Language—reward or cost?

RESPECT

There's an old adage that goes sadly like this: Marriage is a poor substitute for respect.

Respect is the way you demonstrate the value of your partner's life, the way your words and behavior prove the worth of all you share together.

Without mutual respect, your relationship is not between equals. Without respect, ears turn deaf, attitudes sour, and eventually you can't figure out what you're doing living with someone so incompetent, stupid, unreliable, insensitive, emotional, ugly, smelly, untidy. . . . It makes you wonder why you chose your partner in the first place. "I must have been out of my mind."

But with respect, a relationship brings new opportunities. There's so much you can learn from one another. There are so many more experiences you can have because each person enriches the other's life, opens new doors, brings new perspective. You find yourself constantly impressed with the other person's intelligence, thoughtfulness, kindness, sensitivity, beauty, grace, handsomeness. . . . It makes you glad to walk into a room together, arm in arm. "It was my lucky day when I met you."

Respect—reward or cost?

* * *

There are many more relationship qualities, enough to fill a book the size of this one. But now that you have the idea, you can start your own list, one designed especially for your particular intimate relationship.

You might start with *listening, courtesy, tenderness,* and *trust,* which we didn't discuss here. Perhaps your personal list would also include mutual interests like *athletics, books,* or *travel.* Ask your partner for ideas, and for comments. Start a *conversation* and see what new delights you can discover about each other and your intimacy. *Work* can be fun, and the best work is that which we share with someone we love.

CHAPTER 5

INTIMACY BURNOUT

> . . . the young man (or woman) can have only an incomplete understanding of himself and others, and is therefore imperfectly informed as to his, and their, motives. As a rule the motives he acts from are largely unconscious. The greater the area of unconsciousness, the less is marriage a matter of free choice. . . .
>
> —C.G. JUNG
> *Marriage as a Psychological Relationship*

"We've been together too long. There aren't any surprises left."

"It's like all we are now is friends. We go through the motions, but who cares?"

"We're staying together because of our parents."

"We're staying together because of the kids."

"We're staying together because we can't afford a divorce."

* * *

Intimacy burnout becomes apparent when increasing boredom, depression, and resignation settle like lunar dust over an intimate relationship that once was vibrant, exhilarating, pulsating with energy, and so much fun that it crackled with the laughter of the young at heart no matter how old in years.

In intimacy burnout, the draining energy of anxiety replaces the charging energy of discovery.

Most of us have experienced some of these symptoms at one level or another in a relationship. Friendships that were once so promising that just seemed to wither away and die. Love relationships that were like shooting stars for some nights of our lives but that disappeared in the light of day. And profound, committed love relationships that endured and seemed destined to last forever but that also burned out, dying in spectacular, fiery explosions or—more often—expiring slowly from malnutrition and neglect, buried eventually in indifference.

What happens to cause intimacy burnout in this wide spectrum of human relationships? What happens to distance our friends, our parents and children, our lovers, and our husbands or wives? And what can be done to revitalize an ailing relationship so only those relationships that really want and need to die may do so?

* * *

Relationship therapy is not intended to function as a Forest Lawn beautician, making dead relationships look pretty on their way to the grave.

Some relationships do want to die. Some relationships, like some human bodies, do need to find their rest in peace. Some are ill-conceived and should never have begun. Not all marriages are made in heaven.

Good therapy is designed to separate the relationships that need to live and are capable of life from those that need to be allowed to die because they have no life left in them.

Many relationships—friendships, loving relationships, and marriages—appear to be alive and well but have a consuming worm gnawing at the core. Those survive only because of social and financial pressures, or they're propped up by fear and procrastination.

And at the same time, sadly, some relationships break up before they are given a chance to heal and revitalize.

Many relationships listed in newspaper divorce columns should have been trial separations instead. They are taken off the resuscitator even though they aren't terminally ill because too few people know what to do to save them.

In the following chapters we'll take a close look at what causes troubled intimate relationships.

We'll examine ways to detect trouble before it begins to manifest itself.

We'll explore ways in which already troubled relationships can be transformed.

And we'll discuss methods to keep fresh and enduring our vital, intimate relationships.

*   *   *

Barbara and Bill Tinley had been married fourteen years when they came to me with an extreme case of intimacy burnout.

Bill was a certified public accountant, and Barbara a housewife and part-time nurse. Both were in their late thirties. They lived in a luxurious suburban home, had three attractive children, and led a quiet, well-ordered life. They were active in school and community affairs, entertained once or twice a month, and were considered by their friends to be a model couple.

One Monday morning Barbara was going through Bill's jacket pockets, preparing his suits for the cleaners. She discovered a telephone number written on a slip of paper. "That's when I knew it," she told me later. "Everything made sense!"

People have a remarkable ability to pick up the subtle, unspoken clues of an environment. Without consciously acknowledging it, Barbara had been suspicious for several years that Bill had been having sexual relationships with other women. When she found the slip of paper with only the telephone number, all her unrecognized misgivings coalesced.

She dialed the number. "I understand my husband has been seeing you," she told the woman.

Voice shaking with relief, the woman told Barbara about the affair, said she'd often thought of calling her. She said she was deeply in love with Bill and asked Barbara to divorce him.

Cold with fury and betrayal, Barbara said she'd think about it. She hung up. She steeled herself to continue the chores of the day. Without duty, she had little meaning to her life.

She took her husband's clothes to the cleaners, worked several hours at the hospital where she was a nurse in intensive care, picked up the children after school, prepared their dinners and a separate, more elaborate dinner for her and Bill which she kept warm in the oven.

As usual, Bill worked late. She called the office, and he was there. To maintain his successful practice, he worked long, hard hours, often going out for conferences, lunches, and dinners with the important businessmen who were his clients. His irregular hours were a perfect cover.

When at last he arrived home, the children were in bed, the candles were lit on the table, and Barbara was waiting for him. They had a pleasant dinner, went to bed early, and even had sex. "We quit making love years ago," Barbara said later about their sexual relationship. "What are you complaining about?" Bill responded. "You never liked it anyway."

The next morning, as usual, Barbara helped the children off to school. Bill was in the hallway, arranging papers in his briefcase.

From the kitchen, Barbara watched him, inarticulate with humiliation, loathing, and fear.

Then, feeling almost as if she were in a dream, Barbara selected a carving knife from a drawer, walked up to Bill, and stabbed him.

She stabbed him in the chest, not very deep. Instantly she collapsed into tears while he stared dumbfounded as blood spread across his shirt.

The next day they had their first appointment with me.

* * *

The repressed needs of a relationship can erupt into violence. Even in the very nicest, well-bred people, needs that are unrecognized, unspoken, and therefore unmet can kill the source that could have met the needs.

Beware of relationships with placid surfaces, because beneath often seethes frustration and discontent. The resulting distress can kill either overtly with knives and guns, subtly with wounding deeds and words, or covertly with icy aloofness.

Beware, too, of relationships where every conversation ends in an argument, where every crisis must be blamed on someone, where quietness and tranquility are drowned in anger. In this situation, the surface of the relationship is a high-pitched cry for help.

In between these two extremes of intimacy burnout dwells a variety of relationships that are also ailing, but not quite to the degree of the placid relationship and the screaming relationship.

In my practice and in the workshops I conduct I find the primary cause of relationship burnout to be misused, abused stress.

That was the case with Barbara and Bill. In the next three chapters, we will talk more about stress, its causes, its symptoms, and how to use stress instead of its abusing you.

But for now, let's take an overview look at what happened in Bill and Barbara's therapy sessions.

* * *

With prompting, Barbara and Bill Tinley spent their early sessions detailing grievances. Both were experiencing a great deal of pain, anger, and fear, and neither wanted to admit responsibility for their sad relationship. They began with surface comments:

> BILL: I work long hours. I've got three kids to clothe, feed, and educate. I get tense with all the pressure. Every once in a while I need to blow off a little steam. Sex helps. Barbara doesn't like it all that much, so I go elsewhere. What's the big deal? It didn't hurt her when she didn't know about it.

> BARBARA: How could Bill betray me like this? That woman knows everything about us, the secrets of our lives together! I work hard, too. I work a job as well as do all the house things and take care of the kids. I need to blow off steam, too. How would he like it if I went out and had affairs?

Many times Barbara and Bill wanted to quit the dialogs. Their sessions were furious, agonizing, painful, and full of recriminations as they revealed their wounds. Eventually their comments began to probe beneath the surface, and they began talking to each other instead of strictly to me:

BILL: I used to ask you to go with me to conventions and when I had to travel out of town.

We had fun together. Then the kids were born and you wouldn't come. We could have hired babysitters.

It was like I wasn't important anymore. Now that you had kids, I had to go to the end of the line.

BARBARA: They're our kids. You can't leave babies for a week at a time. How would you feel if something happened, an accident? They could have a terrible accident and we wouldn't be here to take care of them. Besides, you were so busy making contacts at those conventions that you didn't have any real time for me. I was horribly bored, but you snapped your fingers and I came anyway.

After much time had passed, Barbara and Bill began to get to the heart of their problems:

BILL: You don't know who I am. All I am to you is a paycheck, someone to nag to pick up the wet towels.

BARBARA: You don't know who I am. All I am to you is a dumb broad tied to the kitchen.

BILL: You don't care who I am. You don't care that I love our children, too. You don't care that even though I know it isn't good enough I'm still trying my hardest. You don't care that even though I didn't learn to show my love the way you learned that I keep trying despite my discouragement.

BARBARA: You don't care who I am. You don't care enough to listen to my opinions, to listen to me with the same respect that you listen to your business friends. You don't care that I'm desperately trying by my hard work to be on equal terms with your work life.

And so the dialog continued for Bill and Barbara.

The period when we blame others lasts a long time. It's understandable after years of abuse and being abused. We hurt one another in innumerable little ways that add up to gigantic, open wounds, and in that sense the blame is justified.

But blame does not heal our wounds. Blame is not a salve; it is an irritant. It only makes us hurt more.

At last after much resistance and hard, painful work facing the unpleasant sides within each of them, Barbara and Bill's dialog began to sound like this:

BILL: Please look at me, know who I am now, today. See me for who I really am. I'm deeply sorry for any hurt I've caused you.

BARBARA: Please look at me, know who I am now, today. See me for who I really am. I'm deeply sorry for any hurt I've caused you.

Finally Barbara and Bill Tinley were talking honestly and meaningfully. It was the first time in years, perhaps the first time in their marriage. Many couples whose relationships have deteriorated to the depths of the Tinleys would not have been able or willing to do this difficult, agonizing work. It is always easier to face other people's demons than it is our own.

But because Bill and Barbara had continued, they began to develop strong senses of who they were, what was really important to each of them, and what they needed for nurturing from an intimate relationship.

As I said before, one of the major purposes of good intimacy therapy is to separate the relationships that need to live and are capable of life from those that need to be allowed to die because they have no life left in them.

Much marriage counseling is divorce counseling in disguise. It's easier for us to say, "We were in marriage counseling but it failed," than it is to say, "We were in divorce counseling and it succeeded."

Real success lies in arriving at the right answer for each individual couple.

In a marriage that wants to live, that has life signs—no matter how faint—success often means revitalizing the relationship so it is once more intimate and fulfilling, with life signs vibrating with good health.

In a dead marriage, or in a marriage where the life signs are becoming more and more feeble until they no longer can be heard, success usually means divorce. But the divorce is accomplished with dignity and understanding so each partner may leave with a minimum of damage and a maximum of information about each of them and what an intimate relationship really is. Armed with this knowledge, they have foundations on which to build the right intimate relationships with new partners.

Bill and Barbara's marriage had been an extreme case of intimacy burnout. But now the relationship showed stirrings of life. At this point there was no way to predict what would happen. However, if they continued their dialogs of self-revelation and vulnerability, and if they discovered it was their desire, I believed they could rebuild their marriage into fulfilling, transforming intimacy. We will talk more about them in greater detail later.

CHAPTER 6

THE STRESS OF BEING ALIVE

> It is the strength of the bond to the parents that uncon-
> sciously influences the choice of husband or wife, either posi-
> tively or negatively. . . . Generally speaking, all the life
> which the parents could have lived, but of which they
> thwarted themselves for artificial motives, is passed on to the
> children in substitute form. That is to say, the children are
> driven unconsciously in a direction that is intended to com-
> pensate for everything that was left unfulfilled in the lives of
> their parents.
>
> —C.G. JUNG
> *Marriage as a Psychological Relationship*

"I don't know what happened to us," Bill Tinley said one day
to me. "I suppose we did it to ourselves, but what did we do?"

"We must have been in love once," Barbara Tinley added. "If
our relationship had been this awful in the beginning, we never
would have married."

In my experience, just as abandonment is the primary fear:

*Abused stress is the primary mechanism with which
we unwittingly cause our relationships to die.*

Once individual and relationship stresses get out of control, less
and less room is left for intimacy to grow, let alone flourish. Because of stress's power, our understanding of it, of distress and of
de-stress, can help us greatly. With knowledge, stress can be a
weapon to use *for* the good of our intimate relationships, not
against them.

* * *

Despite mass publicity to the contrary, stress in itself is not bad for you. In fact, I have a revelation that may startle you:

Stress is necessary and good for all of us.

Many books are written on the evils of stress. Perhaps even more books are written on how to avoid stress. But the only condition in life in which you can avoid stress is death.

Why? Because everyone's life is naturally full of stress. No one can escape it.

- You cannot have a relationship without stress, nor should you. What a bore that would be!

- You cannot have any significant work without stress. Each of us yearns for challenge.

- You cannot read the newspaper, watch television, even walk down the street without stress. We see changes everywhere that need to be made.

Stress is like electricity. If the lights, heat, and stereo are turned off in the room in which you are reading this book, you are probably unaware of the existence of electricity. Nevertheless, electricity is all around you, even appearing in the air you're breathing right now.

When used in a positive way, electricity can illuminate the night, heat the cold, and cook nutritious food for you. But if out of ignorance you were to stick a finger in an electrical socket and turn on the switch, that same neutral electricity could kill you.

Like electricity, stress is all around us, neutrally waiting for us to use its power. With stress, we can light up our lives, or we can ignorantly give ourselves a terrible jolt, one that could send us to the hospital—or the morgue:

Stress is simply a call made by reality for you to change one of your behaviors or attitudes.

Stress can be external, such as personal financial worries, the state of the economy, or the way your friends, family, or boss is treating you.

It can be internal, such as the slow realization your life isn't going where you want it. You may be in the wrong career but so financially strapped (or successful) you're afraid to try something new. You may be in an unhealthy relationship but don't know how to fix it or how to get out of it.

Stress means choices, and it means conflict, because out of conflict comes growth and, yes, the need to make those choices. Reality may be saying to you—

Do something about your job; you're bored and need to find a new challenge.

Do something about your love of music; you miss hearing it in your daily life.

Do something about the broken back gate; some child may wander into the yard and drown in the hot tub.

Do something about the lack of love in your life; you are going to die bitter and alone.

Do something about the wonderful intimacy you have in your life; without appreciation any living thing withers away.

So what do we do about all this stress?

Fortunately, we human beings have a remarkable psychological ability called adaptation. We have the genetic ability to adapt and to change. For us, stress can be like any other useful tool in our lives.

Stress can benefit us greatly. Or stress can destroy us.

We have a choice.

* * *

There are two ways for us to react to stress:

- Distress
- De-stress

When we refuse to change, or when we resist the need and go on our way as if reality were not insisting on our making some adjustments, we move into the powerful and negative energy of distress.

But when we respond to stress by making changes that are right for us, we possess the equally powerful and positive energy of de-stress, which can transform our fears—and therefore, our lives.

Electricity's power can be channeled for good or for ill.

Stress's power can be channeled for good or for ill.

Some stresses are so enormous we shape our lives around them; for instance, the heartbreak of a dying child or spouse.

Other stresses are so small we hardly notice them at all; an example might be a toothbrush worn to the point that maybe it should be replaced.

And in between are a variety of stresses in areas such as career, marriage, family, need for approval, financial security, whom to associate with, religious conviction, where to live, what foods to eat, the time to spend on the various interests in your life, and so forth.

Please think about the stresses in your life.

I suggest you write a list; we'll refer to it later. Give yourself plenty of time to do this.

Once you start to identify your stresses, you also start to identify the threads from which the fabric of your life is woven.

You have the power to make those threads weak or strong through distress or de-stress.

* * *

Suzanne, twenty-eight years old, single and beautiful, arrived in my office for a late session. She was dressed for a movie premiere in a long, sweeping gown. She sparkled with excitement and the potentials of life. To look at her with her lovely face and figure, her gracious manners, and the newfound peace that glowed beneath the excitement, you'd have a hard time imagining the tired, depressed, drawn young woman with whom I'd been working for two years.

In those two years Suzanne had been playing a Ping-Pong game with two men who were her lovers. One was a professional career man, and the other was an attractive young man who found holding a job difficult.

Neither man knew she was seeing the other. She couldn't tell them or choose between them because she was afraid of losing each. Both were very much in love with her, but they were in love with only half-truths about her.

During the two years of therapy she had worked hard and at last successfully to break her addiction to alcohol and cocaine. Now that she had conquered those two demons, she was at last able to confront her addiction to the relationships.

Because she was terrified of losing her two men and the false sense of intimacy the relationships provided, her life was filled with constant anxiety and depression, and so she lived in a state of dishonesty with both.

During our previous session she had said, "How can I live without a relationship?"

"You've been doing that for two years," I said. "You haven't had one."

After more work and thinking in the session, she concluded that by living completely false lives with each man, she really didn't have either.

I suggested her ability to see the relationships so clearly indicated she was strong enough to level with the men.

When she walked into my office that evening for her next session, dressed in her long gown, sparkling with electricity, her first words were "I did it!"

She fell into a chair, triumphant, trembling with the aftereffects of the courage she'd summoned to talk honestly with her lovers.

She had been working against two fears. The first was the fear of losing the two men, who together were the closest relationships to intimacy she had in her lonely life. The second fear was of confronting reality, which she had avoided doing for years in many different areas.

These were pre-revelation fears, the results of her feelings of helplessness, hopelessness, and being trapped. She had avoided the neutral stresses of reality—the need to change—for so long that she had been caught in negative and destructive behavior. This showed in her many symptoms, including anxiety, depression, and the abuse of alcohol and cocaine.

This is classic distress:

Distress is the use of stress's neutral energy in a negative way.

To many people, dealing with stress means repressing it, sweeping it under the rug, pretending it doesn't exist. They want to disengage, walk away. Very frequently, all that does is allow the stress to settle in as chronic, painful, damaging distress, which is what happened to Suzanne, as well as to Barbara and Bill Tinley in their marriage.

In her therapy session tonight Suzanne was showing the signs of positive change. Every aspect of her seemed to sing. She was happy, proud, delighted. Physically she looked different, bright with newness, vibrant, beautiful.

But she said she was also in a state of fear.

It was a new fear for her, one that resulted from taking control of her life. She was being challenged by seeing what life had to offer.

Positive and creative, she was de-stressing.

To look and talk to her you could easily believe her when, despite the new fear, she told you she felt transformed and eager to get on with life.

This is classic de-stress:

De-stress is the use of stress's energy in a positive way.

Soon both relationships ended. Although hurt and saddened, Suzanne was free at last to have a relationship with somebody who would want her because of who she really is, and whom she could want with the growing understanding of what she needs from life.

For the past two years she had been going through the stress of transition. In that time she not only had ended her addiction to cocaine and alcohol, she also had left a dead-end job and returned to school. Soon she found a very good part-time job to help support her while she completely remodeled her life goals. At the top of her list was an honest, intimate relationship, which at last was possible for her.

* * *

The de-stress that is transformational can look like the distress that is destructive. Fear is natural. It isn't necessarily bad, and it can be very good. Fear is one of the ways stress delivers its message to you.

For instance, if I have a fear of failing an examination in school, that fear can propel me into the work that enables me not only to pass the examination but also to do quite well in it.

On the other hand, the fear may terrify me so much that I freeze, become incapable of studying at all, and fail.

And in between is the response to fear in which I do just well enough to pass, but not quite well enough to excel. Remember our earlier discussion of the prison we build when we fear success and failure?

Stress can look like either fear. To discover the difference, ask yourself some questions:

What is the fear saying? What is the message?
What are the choices that the stress appears to offer?
What am I afraid of most?
What do I want most?
What will happen if I succeed?
What will happen if I fail?

What do I really want to do?

You have choices. For instance, you may study, not study, or you may study only a moderate amount.

Your fear is neutral until you decide which choice to make. If you choose action that is right for you, you may fear the challenge, but your life will be changed for the better, transformed. If you choose action that is wrong for you, or if you ignore the necessity to choose, you will still be afraid, and you will suffer the symptoms of distress as well.

Fear is a delivery system for stress.

It carries a message that offers you opportunities for either destruction or transformation.

CHAPTER 7

MAKING THE MOST OF YOUR STRESS

> If the individual is to be regarded solely as an instrument for maintaining the species, then the purely instinctive choice of a mate is by far the best. But since the foundations of such a choice are unconscious, only a kind of impersonal liaison can be built upon them, such as can be observed to perfection among primitives. If we can speak here of a "relationship" at all, it is, at best, only a pale reflection of what we mean, a very distant state of affairs with a decidedly impersonal character, wholly regulated by traditional customs and prejudices, the prototype of every conventional marriage.
>
> —C.G. JUNG
> *Marriage as a Psychological Relationship*

Some twenty years ago I was elected the Anglican bishop of Kimberley, South Africa. I lived in South Africa not very long, a little less than three years, but they were an intense three years, and in them I came to know firsthand the dynamics of extreme stress.

By first accepting the post of dean of the Kimberley cathedral, and then by being elected bishop, I was plunged in depth into the trauma of apartheid in South Africa.

I opposed apartheid.

I invited friends of mine—who also happened to be black—into my home and I dined with them in restaurants, which was against the law. I fought for the right of blacks to move freely in the streets, for their right to be treated in any hospital, for their right to marry whomever they chose, and for their right to vote. Thorough coverage by the international press helped me on one occasion to convince the government to return black people from arid, life-depriving lands where they were dying back to their original lands where they could farm and make their livings.

The government retaliated.

The police stationed cars outside my home around the clock. They photographed anyone who entered or left. They threatened to arrest me if I continued to lead food drives to feed black people who were starving, and indeed they did arrest me many times.

They raided my home, where I lived with my wife and three small children. They seized books from my personal library. The books were ordinary novels and nonfiction works that could be purchased in any United States bookstore at the time. The South African police called them seditious.

Then in 1967 I was invited to Geneva to speak at the Pacem in Terris (Peace on Earth) international conference. Martin Luther King, Jr., asked me to speak on racism while he gave his first speech linking the civil rights movement to the anti–Vietnam War movement.

News photographers took pictures of us together. One was printed on the front pages of South African newspapers.

When the South African prime minister saw the photograph, he was outraged—the white bishop of Kimberley was working and cooperating with an outspoken, powerful black leader who symbolized freedom to blacks around the world.

The minister ordered documents drawn up that forbade my return, and he told the press I was "the most hated man in all Africa." I went back to South Africa anyway. I was arrested. A week later they deported me. My family followed shortly afterwards.

At the Kimberley airport, police with attack dogs weaved among a crowd of several thousand—mostly blacks and "coloreds," but some whites, too—who had gathered on the tarmac. These people were my parishioners, the police as well as the crowd. Yet they were on the verge of violence. Many in the crowd had traveled for days on foot because they had heard I must go. The police let me speak to them, and I talked about peace and racial justice. In response, they wept and sang songs of South Africa.

How could I leave? There was still so much work left undone! I was put on the plane.

Nietzsche has written, " 'Tis night. Now do all fountains speak louder. And my soul also is a bubbling fountain." I had invested everything I emotionally, intellectually, physically, and morally possessed into helping free the wonderful country of South Africa from the evils of apartheid. Reality was calling for massive changes in that nation, and I was doing my best to respond. The people there had come to call me "the voice of the voiceless." But now I was expelled, powerless. I felt empty, and alone. It was a long, dark night for my soul.

I had to take a new look at my situation—at the intense stress I experienced in South Africa dealing with the people and the issues of apartheid, and then at the heartbreaking stress of deportation.

This was my first real understanding of stress and my resulting distress. I was hit head-on by it, a blow like a Mack truck slamming into a concrete wall.

I knew stress was either going to destroy me, or transform me.

Somehow I also knew that despite my feelings of inadequacy and powerlessness, I could make choices.

I chose to transform. The other option was unacceptable.

I didn't know then I would actually be able to transform, and that many of my later choices when involved in other stressful, painful situations would continue to enrich and strengthen my life.

And so I traveled for a year and a half, talking around the globe to anyone who would listen. I worked in many countries with the growing anti-apartheid movement, trying to educate people about the evils of prejudice and racism. On two occasions I addressed the United Nations. Then I settled with my family in California as a fellow at the Center for the Study of Democratic Institutions, which examined world politics and peace. And at last, seeking a new way to work with people, I returned to school and got a doctorate in counseling psychology.

As I write this, I marvel at how easily the events seem to fall into natural alignment. *Of course I would do that then. Of course I would do this later.* I write too easily of events always full of questions, often full of agony, sometimes full of great pride and happiness. *Was this right? Was that right? What to do? Had I done everything I could do?*

And there were private human problems involved, a family to consider, children to help grow to adulthood, and eventually—sadly—a divorce.

It has been a rocky, difficult, stress-filled road for me, but probably on a deeper level no more difficult or easy than for anyone else. I am grateful for the opportunity to have walked my road, to still be wondering what is around the next bend. It has brought me to a new place I never could have envisioned in my youth, and yet it is a familiar place, one I have always known.

* * *

Stress offers me choices. Stress offers you choices. Choices open doors to unexpected possibilities.

Once we begin to see the wealth of possibilities that choice means, stress becomes a less fearful word. The years will pass anyway. How much better for all of us to pass those years walking our own individual roads, and they will be the right roads for us if we use stress as a tool.

* * *

The thirty-five-year-old woman sat quietly in the chair in my office. Her skin color was tinged with gray. Her eyes were dull. She wore an expensive dark wool business suit and pumps. Her briefcase was at her feet. Ordinarily she spoke with firm authority, but today her voice was shaking.

"I thought it was a heart attack," she said. "They ran all the tests at the hospital. They said there's nothing wrong with my heart. They said I was having an anxiety attack. An anxiety attack? Me? How could that be?"

Distress is like an equal opportunity employer. It is blind to race, sex, age, or occupation. It has only one rule—if you don't deal with your stress, your stress will deal with you. And that means the ugly consequences of distress.

Distress shows itself primarily in three areas:

- Our bodies
- Our emotions
- Our behaviors

The first step toward healing is for you to identify your distress symptoms. Remember, you're not alone. All of us inevitably have symptoms of distress.

Even though my new client said she didn't know how she could have had an anxiety attack, she had been having them regularly for years. As we talked, she discovered her history of brief periods of clammy hands, short breath, eventually her heart pounding hard. She had ignored the small attacks even as they grew larger, more powerful. Then came the big attack that sent her to the hospital in great pain and terrified she was dying.

Now her stress had her attention. Her Mack truck had slammed into her concrete wall.

Think about your distress symptoms, even the small ones. Once you're aware of them, you can begin to trace them back, relate them to events and people, especially look for their origins in your personal stresses and the stresses in your relationships.

The following are common symptoms often rooted in distress or aggravated by distress:

PHYSICAL SYMPTOMS—Stomach aches, sexual dysfunction, heartburn, grinding teeth, asthma, respiratory disorders, heart disease, ulcers, lower and upper back pains, neck pains, headaches, migraines, nervous tics, rashes, skin eruptions, insomnia, constipation, diarrhea, twitching, loss of appetite.

EMOTIONAL SYMPTOMS—Depression; anxiety; phobias; sudden eruptions of anger, weird attitudes, and dislikes; the need to be taken care of like a child; the need for compensatory aggression.

BEHAVIOR SYMPTOMS—Alcoholism; workaholism; smoking; addiction to drugs such as cocaine, heroin, tranquilizers, and sleeping pills; overeating; anorexia nervosa; bulimia; addiction to gambling; episodic violence.

* * *

Inevitably, how we handle our stress affects our intimate relationships. Conversely, lack of intimacy is one of the major causes of stress.

If you unconsciously program yourself to translate the stress in your life into physical channels, you will have physical symptoms. Most people have some physical symptoms of stress. In the United States we spend hundreds of millions of dollars annually treating the symptoms of distress, trying to buy good health.

Sickness has a big payoff in our society. As children, we learn we can avoid homework, housework, or going to school if we are sick. As adults, we get free medical insurance if we work for a large corporation or the government. In other employment, we often get a few days off with pay to be sick. Illnesses yield sympathy and attention; being physically incapacitated is socially acceptable, often even rewarding.

Increasingly scientific studies show distress may play an important part in other illnesses such as the common cold, influenza, and even cancer. Scientists theorize that distress weakens our immune systems, paving the way for us to offer hospitality to disease.

Probably the most obvious and primary dumping ground for distress is in emotional symptoms. Depression is a fact of life for many of us, the kind of depression that you cannot seem to shake. Most of us experience it in its moderate state, not ill to the point of being immobilized, but depressed enough that every thought and movement requires twice as much energy as we think it should.

There are basically two kinds of depression:

- Reactive depression
- Endogenous depression

A reactive depression happens because you are reacting to something bad that has happened outside you. For instance, someone close to you has died, or you're going through a divorce, or you've just been fired. It also can be as simple as something rotten happening that disillusions you about human nature, and then you realize you're a part of the human race, and that thought depresses you. All of this is reactive depression.

In endogenous depression, the depression comes from inside. This is difficult to deal with because there's no obvious reason for the depression, although a stress or two are probably at its heart. When it hits, you may not know what has happened to you. Everything in your external life may seem wonderful, but suddenly you're sunk in a deep depression. You don't know how to get out of it. You feel helpless, hopeless, and out of control. You are indeed distressed.

And then the depression has physical consequences. You lose your appetite. You can't sleep. So you take an extra drink at night, a strong one, or you resort to sleeping pills. The symptoms of distress feed one another, too frequently leading to addictions.

We now know that distress is a component of both major depression and anxiety. Just as depression pulls you down, anxiety pushes you up. Depression is a pricked balloon, and anxiety is filling the balloon until it bursts. Many of us have anxiety attacks. Our hands grow clammy, our hearts begin to palpitate, we start to hyperventilate, our insides feel as shaky as gelatin. Unpleasant and frightening, anxiety, too, is deeply rooted in distress.

In distress, the more inferior we feel, the more aggressive will be our compensatory behavior. We try to prove to ourselves that we are not as inadequate as we secretly believe. This kind of conflict causes tremendous distress. Most of us resist identifying it because we don't like to think such things about ourselves. But until it is identified and dealt with, it will continue to afflict our lives and our relationships.

Many people suffer from behavioral problems as well. We learn to hide our stresses behind socially acceptable masks. For instance, a workaholic is rewarded with the trappings of success—

money, power, and the envy of peers. When we see or read about movie stars and other celebrities who get drunk, smoke cigarettes or marijuana, and snort lines of cocaine, those damaging behaviors take on a patina of glamour.

That makes it easier for us to ignore the long-range consequences of addiction and physical abuse, and the crossover effects where an emotional symptom causes a physical symptom, a physical symptom triggers a behavioral symptom, a behavioral symptom erupts in an emotional symptom, and so forth.

Distress can become an endless, vicious, chronic cycle in which the monsters of our distress grow so big and powerful that we think we can never beat them.

No wonder our intimate relationships can become the victims of our distresses.

* * *

"It's like a nightmare," the young man told me. "I can't stop talking. Every time I go out on a date, it's the same thing. I talk, talk, talk! Sometimes I drink too much. I bore my date, and I bore myself!"

He's also found a way to hide from the stress of the intimacy of communicating with another person. His distress shows in his behavior—particularly the compulsive, nonstop talking—which makes a two-way conversation impossible. And then the distress feels so bad to him that he drinks, hoping to feel better.

Most distress symptoms are born in our pasts. Each of us carries various scripts that, like stuck records, replay old ways of masking problems. For instance, a friend's insulting remark may send one person to the bar for a drink.

The same insulting remark may send another person into a deep depression. That remark may cause a third person to punch the friend in the nose.

We all react differently to hurt and pain. But still, we react. Why? Because our old scripts carry damaging self-descriptive messages like:

I am: Unlovable
Unworthy
Inadequate
Useless
Ugly
Fat
Incompetent
Insensitive
Stupid
Overwhelmed
Sinful
Crazy
Untrustworthy
Irresponsible
Helpless
A Failure
Phony

Do any of these words sound like the unspoken, inner fears you have about yourself? We can learn to change the scripts based on these messages. We wrote some of the scripts ourselves. Some were written for us, often by people long dead. Some were written by society.

A source of tremendous but potentially useful stress in our lives is the need to change our various scripts.

Because of the power of the messages' conditioning on us, we find difficulty looking at ourselves in new, positive terms that are more real than the old recorded scripts. We may have earned five million dollars in the last ten years and be financially comfortable for life, but if our script reads "incompetent," we will find ways to make ourselves miserable despite the evidence of our competence.

As you think about the words I've listed, consider your emotional reaction to each.

Are two or three—or even more—familiar self-accusations?

If you have a negative, worried reaction to any of them, no matter how slight, you're close to answers for yourself.

Once you've identified a few of the messages as may be applicable to you, reflect on them and their meanings.

Try to understand where each came from. Who or what was the origin? How did each message continue to live and grow until it became one of your life scripts?

Just by examining each message honestly and thoughtfully, you will drain its power. The negative aspects of us thrive in the dark. Once exposed to the light of recognition and evaluation, they dwindle and eventually can be put to rest.

Examine how the meaning of each word is reflected in different parts of your life now. Decide what you can do to counteract the messages. With those messages that you think you can do little about, you place yourself in a victim role. Ask yourself very seriously why you have to remain a victim.

Just as you have the choice to accept or reject these destructive scripts, you also have the choice to face the stresses that originated them.

Like Suzanne's triumph over her drug abuse problems and being honest about her two partial love affairs, you also can choose to change, to transform your life. You can channel your stress into the transformational power of de-stress. And then you can apply your newfound self-knowledge to the stresses and distresses in your relationships.

* * *

In my many years of being a psychotherapist and having the privilege of working with a variety of people and their problems, I have not become embittered, disillusioned, or pessimistic about the human condition.

Quite the contrary. I know from experience that each of us has the capacity to produce spiritual, emotional, and physical resurrection from many different forms of death. We can transform what can destroy us into something that can transfigure us.

In the preceding chapter I asked you to consider the stresses in your life. You made a mental list or you wrote them down. Now I'd like you to compare that stress list with the word-messages that we've just been talking about.

Do you notice that your choices of stresses and scripted messages seem to fit together?

That's no accident. If you wrote "marriage" as a major stress in your life, and if you chose "unlovable" and "phony" from the list of words, you are getting a strong hint that your feelings of being unlovable and a phony are affecting your relationship with your husband or wife.

In fact, the meanings of those words in your life script may have led you to choose the wrong partner for marriage in the first place. On the other hand, they may have prompted you unconsciously to choose a person you knew could help you to transform them into positive energies, if you will only allow this to happen.

If you also wrote "job" as one of your major stresses, then your view of yourself as unlovable and a phony is going to affect your relationships with your fellow workers, your boss, and the employees who work under you.

If you feel so unlovable that you are also unlikable, you may become a petty tyrant in order to compensate, or an ineffectual pushover to try to attract the emotional attention you need.

And if you feel like a phony, no matter how good a job you do you will always be waiting to fail because all phonies know that eventually they will be discovered for the shams they are.

It seems endless, doesn't it? But it needn't be.

You can make your stress work for you.

Others have done it, myself included, and so can you.

* * *

To begin your transformation from distress to de-stress, rate your stresses on a Richter scale of 1 through 10. Give a 10 to the biggest, scariest, most overwhelming, explosive stresses in your life. Give a 1 to the most minor, trivial ones.

Look at those 9s and 10s and be grateful.

The good news is the most powerful stresses—the 9s and 10s —offer the greatest opportunity for your freedom—transformation.

The bad news is they also carry more pain than do smaller stresses. And that's what we back off from—pain.

But consider this: we can be fairly sure the pain of physically dying because of the symptoms of distress is greater than the pain of resurrection through de-stress.

It's the pain of death compared to the pain of birth.

I think the pain of birth is more tolerable because it has a conscious future to it.

Remember Charlie and Kate who together conquered his need to test intimate relationships? His testing was a behavioral symptom of distress. The stress of intimacy became a 10 on his Richter scale. The distress was rooted in his fear of abandonment. But after much painful work he de-stressed, transformed, and now has what he believed was impossible for him—a solid, loving, intimate relationship with Kate. Remember my friend Jerry who discovered the important quality that his life had been lacking? In the last few weeks of his life as his body died from cancer, his mind and spirit de-stressed, and he blossomed in timeless intimacy.

Consider Barbara and Bill Tinley, who avoided the distresses of their individual lives and the distresses of their relationship until one revelation—one little scrap of paper with a single telephone number on it—exploded their existence, and she stabbed him. They were lucky. The physical, emotional, and mental damage to both of them was repairable. And with honest, painful examination they transformed a wretched situation into one that offered options.

And think about me, hounded by police, expelled from a country I had grown to love, never to see many dear friends again, my mind and body profoundly distressed. I decided to de-stress, to respond to the demands for change that reality was making. Returning to South Africa would have meant the end of my freedom and, I suspect, my life. So I continued to work for my beliefs elsewhere, learning awkwardly to shift with my needs, with the needs of others, and with the times. Today my children are adult and successful, I have a remarkable and intimate relationship with my wife, Ingrid, and I have work that is deeply satisfying to me. I am grateful for the stresses of my life.

* * *

There's no secret to making your stress work for you. Some people go through life doing it naturally. The rest of us have to learn by living.

You are reading about the learning process in this book. The people in crisis on these pages are experiencing a variety of stresses, distresses, and de-stresses as they search for the intimate relationships that are the right of every human being.

To create the process that is best for you, pay attention to the distresses in your life—where you hurt.

Think about them.

Talk about them to someone who knows how to listen.

Discuss your options.

Decide what is best for you.

And then, painful as it is, do it.

Remember the old adage that the fire that destroys can also forge. Every person is born with the ability to be intimate and to make changes. Use your natural abilities. Forge yourself into the person you were meant to be. Go through the fires of change into the bright new world of transformation.

CHAPTER 8

THE STRESSES OF INTIMACY

Seldom or never does a marriage develop into an individual
relationship smoothly and without crises. There is no birth of
consciousness without pain.

—C.G. JUNG
Marriage as a Psychological Relationship

Pauline Arden and Eric Hansen were in their late twenties, an
attractive couple who had been married a little over a year when
they came to see me.

Each had a career and healthy ambitions. They planned to
have children after both were more established in their professions.
Then they would reduce their work loads to share the responsibilities and joys of raising a family. They were committed to their
marriage; it was vital to both their lives.

"We don't know what's wrong," Eric began.

"We started out so well," Pauline said.

"We were careful," he said. "We discussed everything first.
What our lives were like before, how to compromise, the changes
we'd have to make once we got married."

"I can't imagine we missed anything," she said. "But it's not
working out."

They looked at me, avoiding the pain in each other's eyes.
Their future was in jeopardy, and neither knew what to do.

"My parents were divorced when I was fifteen," Eric said.

"Mine are still married," Pauline added, "but they haven't
spoken a civil word to each other in years."

* * *

In all the agonizing, surgical processes that one has to go through in growing oneself up, facing the stresses of intimacy is probably the hardest. It's no wonder we repress the stress as deeply as possible, and then the relationship—no matter how new or how long-standing—gets distressed, starts to fail, and eventually can die.

Eric and Pauline, because of the thoughtful preparation they had made before marrying, were aware earlier than many of us that something was wrong in their relationship. Because of their parents' marital histories, they knew and dreaded the consequences of dead intimacy. A modern, well-educated couple, they wanted to stop trouble before it became deeply ingrained, and they wanted to recapture their earlier love and harmony.

"Recapturing" was a good place for them to begin their work. Nothing that remains static is healthy. Life means change.

We are meant to grow with the changes—with the stresses. That's one of the reasons we have the built-in ability to adapt.

Those of us who keep trying to recapture the past are doomed. It is impossible, and the attempt only adds to our misery.

The peak of happiness for Eric and Pauline had been their wedding day. They rightly felt they had earned the perfection of that moment, and that's what each now dreamed of returning to.

Accompanying their conviction was the idea that most of the hard work on their relationship was behind them. Many of us marry with this erroneous thought, the act of wedding somehow erasing any need for future meaningful participation.

Pauline and Eric believed they had arranged their future carefully. They knew exactly where they were going.

Then life surprised them. They met reality and its accompanying stresses.

She hung her panty hose to drip-dry over the shower door. He left his washcloth in a wet wad in the sink.

He hated casseroles. She hated frozen dinners.

She preferred one dry cleaners; he another.

She gave herself a large clothing allowance. He was frugal.

These were minor irritations, the kind they had prearranged to work out.

But then, suddenly, inexplicably, the irritations inflated, constellated. They took on significances far beyond their realities.

Pauline and Eric's minor differences grew crucial, charged with hurt feelings, anger, misunderstanding, and resentment.

They gritted their teeth and compromised. They made uneasy, sullen agreements, and they didn't know why their negotiations weren't full of the sense of satisfaction and happiness they had expected. Reality was shattering their idea of perfection. Stress—the neutral call to make changes and accommodations—had inevitably entered their life-style, and they had translated the stress of intimacy into a distress they had not been able to foretell.

No wonder they wanted to return to the uncomplicated happiness of their wedding day. What they didn't realize was even greater happiness was available to them by forging ahead into the future. Once they learned the language of intimacy, once they learned to use stress as a launching pad to transformational destress, they would have two constant skills with which they could meet life's changing demands.

Eventually their discussions began to end in arguments. They quit talking. Slowly the division between them widened into a gulf. At last they decided to seek professional help.

* * *

Pauline and Eric were right to be concerned about the changes in their relationship. They were forming relationship distresses that if not remedied could settle in as chronic distress.

In counseling, they began to see that each of them—as many of us do—had brought very real, fundamental differences to their relationship. She was generally more liberal and flamboyant; he was more conservative. She was more optimistic; he was more cautious. Although he didn't go to church, he was quietly religious; she believed that this life was all there was, so they'd darn well better make the most of it.

They didn't realize that while they were outwardly negotiating minor differences like where to hang the wet panty hose overnight, and what to do about the wadded washcloth in the sink, they were also negotiating their philosophies and views of life, and the way their internal messages had scripted their views of themselves (Remember "phony," "incompetent," "unlovable," and so forth?).

The result was intimacy stress.

We can avoid deep, important issues with someone we stay with only occasionally. The panty hose and the wadded washcloth can be ignored when we see them only once a week.

But once we live together, the daily dripping panty hose, the daily soggy washcloth, and the other daily annoyances take on a frightful permanency.

And so, when Eric said to Pauline, "Can't you find a better place to hang your panty hose?"—the conservative side of him was silently saying, "I'm concerned my friends will come in here and see your underwear. That makes me uncomfortable,"—and the message with which his inner voice was unconsciously warning him was, "Careful. You're so stupid that you're going to screw up and she'll leave you."

When Pauline said to Eric, "Can't you hang your washcloth on the rack where it belongs?"—the flamboyant side of her was also silently saying, "I bought these wonderful colorful towels and washcloths because they make the bathroom look dashing, daring. It makes me unhappy not to have them hanging the way I envisioned,"—and the message her inner voice was unconsciously repeating was, "Watch it, before you know it he'll see how unartistic and unworthy you are, and then he won't want you any more."

They negotiated what they saw, and what they saw was the seemingly unimportant habits that appeared to be causing friction between them.

The preferences and messages underneath went unnoticed and unsaid.

Without knowing it, they translated what was undealt with into hurt feelings, frustration, and at last anger.

Ironically, the more they apparently succeeded in resolving their problems, the more unhappy and hurt each became because the real differences were being ignored.

The opportunities stress was offering for each to be intimate—to reveal his or her personal motivations—were being passed over.

The practical side of the negotiations was uppermost in each one's mind. They were adhering to their formula, their plan. That was the way each had achieved past successes.

But their plan did not take into account the need for intimacy's revelations because Pauline and Eric thought, quite simply, that the euphoria of their premarital state was intimacy. Euphoria is part of intimacy, but not all of intimacy.

For Eric and Pauline, their original plan was the only lifeboat in sight. Determined, they stayed aboard, even though the lifeboat was inadequate, unsafe, and wouldn't hold the real weight of the relationship.

Once the surface of the negotiations was peeled away, once they saw they were deeper, more complex, and interesting people than each had thought himself or herself to be, they began to understand why their so carefully planned negotiations had failed.

They began to de-stress, transform.

They allowed themselves to be vulnerable in a new way. They discovered and began to disclose their inner messages and desires. They were talking a new language—the language of intimacy—and with that skill they found they could explore who each of them really was.

Now instead of anger and frustration, their negotiations were filled with exciting revelations. They felt safe telling each other the secrets and fears of their lives, and they learned to value their differences and then incorporate them into their marriage. This is a very intimate thing to do.

They weren't with me very long, just long enough to reenter their marriage on this new road. Life was still unpredictable for them, but now they saw that by using stress—instead of distress abusing them—they could turn that unpredictability into a vehicle for exciting, satisfying change and growth.

* * *

When we think of Eric and Pauline, Barbara and Bill Tinley, Kate and Charlie with Charlie's testing disease, and Suzanne, we can see the merging of two fundamental patterns:

- Every human being needs intimacy, but often we do not have it to the degree we need it.
- Stress is conflict, reality's demand that we pay attention, make changes.

The result?

- The need for intimacy creates a primary stress in life.

Although Eric and Pauline had not been able to respond directly to the distresses they were feeding into their marriage, they were able to respond to their basic need for intimacy.

Because of their family histories, they unconsciously realized the need for intimacy was a primary stress in each of their lives. They wanted to make changes to achieve intimacy, but they did not know what or how.

Unfortunately many of us ignore our needs for intimacy. We get more and more distressed. Our symptoms pile up, growing increasingly annoying, unhealthy, chronic, and eventually very destructive. Inevitably we lead sad, lonely lives as well.

But if we respond to our needs for intimacy, if we allow ourselves to share our autonomy and be vulnerable, then we reward ourselves with both:

- Intimacy's transforming and fulfilling experience

and

- De-stress's transforming and challenging experience

It all seems so simple. But alas, we humans are a contrary lot. Perhaps it is our blessing, too. Once knowingly earned, the power of intimacy is never taken lightly. It is enjoyed and cherished for the work of art it is.

* * *

In the preceding chapter, we talked about how to use a Richter scale of stress to detect those places in your life where you have the greatest chance of painful self-destruction or of life-enhancing transformation. A 2 is an almost unnoticeable temblor. A 5 shakes us and makes us run for shelter. A 9 or 10 can destroy us.

When Pauline and Eric first came to me, they individually decided their distressed marriage rated a 7 on their personal Richter stress scales.

When Barbara and Bill Tinley came to see me, they rated their moribund marriage a massive, explosive 10.

When working with any couple with an ailing intimate relationship, I find helpful an additional scale—a Richter scale of fulfillment:

On a scale of 1 to 10—1 meaning least fulfillment, and 10 meaning greatest fulfillment—how do you rate your primary relationship in terms of life fulfillment?

When considered thoughtfully, this can be an eye-opening question. Obvious as it seems, we often do not stop to think about how fulfilling or unfulfilling we find our primary relationship—we're much too busy getting through life to think about things like that.

But if our primary intimate relationship is central to our existence—to our busy living—then it deserves consideration and time for reflection.

If our intimate relationship is to nourish and transform our spirits, minds, emotions, and bodies, it in turn must be nourished by our attention.

Even if your answer is 1—very unfulfilling—you have succeeded.

The purpose is to answer the question honestly, for out of honesty comes hope and the opportunity for healthy growth.

The question I'm posing is not simple, something to which you can casually toss off a quick answer. Just as I ask all the couples I work with, I ask you now to really think about it, mull it over in your mind:

On a scale of 1 to 10, how do you rate your primary relationship in terms of life fulfillment?

* * *

After your careful consideration of that major question, the next step is easier. On the same scale of fulfillment, now rate the various aspects of your primary intimate relationship, areas such as:

Intimacy
Sex
Children
Family
Conversation
Vacations
Decision making
Companionship
Consideration
Money
Careers
Hobbies
Home buying
Car buying
Recreation

Please give each serious thought. Perhaps you will add other aspects, ones that are integral to your special relationship—like sports, music, philanthropy, or education. The more the better, because by taking a close look at the areas that make up your intimate relationship, you will develop a detailed overview of the topography, of its potential stresses.

For instance, early in my sessions with Bill and Barbara

Tinley, Bill gave his marriage a 10 when he thought of childcare. He felt Barbara was doing a terrific job raising the children.

But Barbara Tinley gave her marriage only a 5 for childcare.

She felt exhausted, inadequate, and that the children needed much more attention than she was able to allot them in her busy day. She thought Bill should participate more.

In financial security, Barbara gave the marriage a 10. She had confidence in Bill and his career, and didn't even consider her part-time nurse's salary significant enough to figure into her tally.

Bill, however, rated the marriage a 4 in financial security. He worried he would get sick and could no longer continue his CPA practice, or that one day all his clients would leave him. Then what would he do? He believed Barbara could never make enough to support them comfortably and send the children through college.

After successfully—and almost as divergently—rating other areas of their lives together, they finally reached the issue of intimacy. I asked each how they would rate the marriage in that area. Now they were hesitant, unsure. Intimacy was not part of their vocabulary. They didn't know what it meant, so how could they evaluate it?

After a lengthy discussion, each decided they rated their marriage only a 1 for intimacy. The rating was a revelation to them, and so was their complete agreement on it. And once they understood what intimacy was, each realized they had been unconsciously searching for it.

The symptoms of the lack of intimacy in their relationship, and the distress that arose from the vacuum, showed particularly in Bill's numerous affairs and in Barbara's cold, methodical way of organizing her life.

Bill's search for love with other women was genuine. He chose women he could fall partly in love with. Unfortunately, he caused them great pain because they fell in love with the Bill they knew. When he abandoned them—and he always did—they were stunned and hurt. But like Suzanne with her lovers, he had showed his lovers only part of himself, and so they were in love with a myth.

When he had to choose between continuing his affairs and trying to revitalize his marriage to Barbara, he was ready to choose revitalizing the marriage. By the time he had come to me, he had already discovered his affairs did not give him lasting happiness. He was marking time, refining excuses for the way he lived—for avoiding stress, the call for change in his life.

Barbara's orderly existence was a method many of us choose to hide from stress. If we can make everything on the outside appear smooth, tranquil, easy to manage—in other words, under our control—then it's easier to convince ourselves everything is fine. No stress in sight. That if there's a problem, it can be remedied by remodeling the kitchen, replacing the sofa or refrigerator, having a baby, changing jobs, schools, wardrobes, even getting a divorce.

We grow veneers of respectability. We surround ourselves in the comfort and security of whatever we can afford to buy. Then we retreat into our havens, which quickly become our prisons, and we die quiet deaths of desperation, still pretending we're in control of our lives.

That's when Barbara chose the kitchen knife from the drawer and stabbed Bill.

Barbara's violence—her act of desperation—terrified and shocked both Bill and Barbara. Suddenly the face of their marriage had radically changed. Neither recognized the relationship, the other person, or even himself or herself.

Bill didn't want to take his own wife to the police. It seemed dishonorable to him, and he worried about the publicity. Besides, she was sobbing uncontrollably. A hysterical woman. Who would believe she was dangerous? He didn't believe she was, but then he would never have thought she would stab him.

He cleaned the wound, using the medical supplies Barbara kept on hand in the upstairs bathroom. When he was finished, he collapsed in a chair in the living room. He shook, frightened, from head to toe. What had happened to Barbara? He guessed, and he didn't like his answer.

That's where Barbara found him. She stood in the doorway, red-eyed, red-faced, a few silent tears still trickling down her cheeks. She didn't know whether to pack her bags, or run for it. Or maybe get the knife and try again.

They didn't speak for quite a while. This was their pattern of respectability. Silence, they thought, kept problems at bay. But this was no ordinary problem.

"Why?" he said at last.

She was quiet. The aching place deep within her told her this time she would have to speak. This situation was too grave to be smoothed over. In a halting voice she told him about finding the telephone number, her call to his lover.

"Do you want a divorce?" she said. She felt relief asking the question. She should have asked it last night. They should have talked last night.

He looked down at his chest, at the bulge of bandages beneath his shirt. He sighed. She'd finally found out, but he'd never thought she'd take it this way. She'd shocked him with her passion.

"I don't know," he said.

Lost, unsure, their furies temporarily stunned into quietness by Barbara's violence, they decided they needed professional help. Bill made the appointment.

The next day they came to my office. The shock of what had happened was wearing off. They were almost inarticulate with anger, betrayal, and self-righteousness. Each wanted me to fix the other.

No one can "fix" another human being. It is the privilege and responsibility of each of us to heal and grow ourselves. But we don't have to do it alone. Often the best help comes from our beloved partner, the man or woman with whom we share our intimate lives.

But Barbara and Bill had no one, and so they needed outside help. Like Pauline and Eric, they needed to learn the language of intimacy.

They began by talking about their present major problems. They made the decision to continue living together during therapy, unless divorce became inevitable. After a few sessions, Bill agreed to end all outside relationships while they worked on their marriage.

As their dialogs progressed, Barbara and Bill made many discoveries. One of them was that each was satisfied by different amounts of fulfillment in the various areas of their marriage.

They learned they didn't always have to want the same amount of satisfaction in the same thing, but that they needed to talk about it until they both had a degree of comfortableness.

Each of us is different, and each of us has different needs. On the Richter scale of fulfillment, some people are satisfied with a 2 or 3 in one area, while others are extremely unhappy with anything less than a 7.

Once stress is addressed, the hidden motivations and messages examined, and each partner satisfied, then the numbers fall away and the fulfillment stands alone, no longer an issue. The potentially damaging situation is transformed into happy, healthful growth.

As Bill and Barbara talked, their personal distresses slowly revealed themselves, and the texture of the distresses in their relationship became more apparent.

They learned that while they were apparently fighting about Bill's love affairs and Barbara's coldness, they were also arguing about deeper issues such as each person's self-worth, hopes for happiness, and fears of insecurity, rejection, and abandonment.

They began to understand the differences in their personalities and the differences caused by those important inner messages that scripted the way they viewed themselves, their individual lives, and their life together.

Thus together they engaged in building a map of their relationship, a topographical guide through the pitfalls of distress to the goal of a de-stressed, transforming, intimate relationship.

CHAPTER 9

THE THIRD PERSON IN INTIMACY

> It is an almost regular occurrence for a woman to be wholly contained, spiritually, in her husband, and for a husband to be wholly contained, emotionally, in his wife. One could describe this as the problem of the "contained" and the "container."
>
> —C.G. JUNG
> *Marriage as a Psychological Relationship*

Intimate relationships—elusive, desired, feared, manipulated, misunderstood, cherished, neglected, withered, fruitful, and euphoric.

At the heart of the adolescent passionate relationship is distressful turbulence. At the heart of the truly adult, passionate relationship is de-stressful peace.

A TWA pilot once told me of the awesome serenity of flying at 45,000 feet, of knowing that beneath him a hurricane stormed while he flew in sunshine and peaceful skies. He compared this high flight to the sexual experience of adult love; he was flying above the turbulence of adolescent passion as he moved toward the serene heart of mature love and passion.

As teenagers, we flail and fume in our search for intimacy.

As adults, the turbulence fades in importance as the consummation of what we seek—intimacy—becomes primary.

Adult passion is deep, continuous. It does not need turbulence to draw attention to itself, nor does it use artificial excitement to pretend it is fulfilling.

As George Bernard Shaw wrote in *Getting Married,* "When two people are under the influence of the most violent, most insane, most delusive, and most transient of passions, they are required to swear that they will remain in that excited, abnormal, and exhausting condition continuously until death do them part." Highly unrealistic, yet many people in our society expect this. No wonder so many distressful relationships die in fiery eruptions of accusations and disappointment.

Turbulence does not nurture and satisfy serenity. Likewise, turbulence is destructive excitement, while serenity is creative excitement—revelations and new ways of viewing life, as my pilot friend saw so clearly at 45,000 feet altitude.

A lasting, deeply satisfying, adult intimate relationship sounds something like this:

> Our intimacy transforms the two of us in our relationship above that which we can ever be alone, and in the transformation it fulfills us beyond our most visionary expectations.

* * *

To help people achieve an intimate relationship that will fulfill this basic goal, I find it useful to give the relationship the same respect and consideration I give a flesh-and-blood person, in fact to consider the relationship to be a person.

After all, we've been talking about relationships as if they were people. They ail, or they are healthy. They have emotional attributes such as happiness and sadness. They can grow or decline. Like an infant exploring the environment, they can develop tools to unlock the mysteries of their world—intimacy. And they are greater than the sum of the parts of the two people who created them. In this equation, one plus one does not equal two, it equals three. Our intimate relationships have births, lives, and deaths of their own.

So I suggest that there are three people in a marriage or in any relationship.

There is Joe Jones.

There is Mary Smith.

And there is the third person—the Jones-Smiths.

Unfortunately, this third person is often the most ignored person in psychotherapy. Treating Joe and Mary individually will not necessarily heal the relationship's ailments. The Jones-Smiths also must be treated.

There are two major sources of distress in the third person—the Jones-Smiths—of intimate relationships:

- The relationship itself
- The individuals in the relationship

* * *

In an intimate relationship, sometimes Joe and Mary are fairly okay as individuals apart. But if Joe is nitrogen and Mary is glycerin, when they come together Mary and Joe make dynamite. That can cause crippling distress in a relationship:

"How come when we're together I drink too much?"

"I never behave like this when I'm with anybody else."

"Why do I make a fool of myself around you?"

"Everyone at the office thinks I'm a really neat person. How can you call me an insulting name like that?"

Dynamite is a radically different element from its two constituent parts, which separately are usually benign. Nitrogen is indispensable to life, and glycerin is a healing agent. But when the two are joined in a certain consistency within a certain environment and shaken up a bit, the result can be explosive.

Unless some changes are made, the third person in this troubled intimate relationship is doomed to distress symptoms. It could be that Joe and Mary are fine, but the Jones-Smiths are sick. The Jones-Smiths are depressed. The Jones-Smiths are filled with anxiety. The Jones-Smiths have behavioral problems. The Jones-Smiths are unruly, addictive, dependent, destructive, even lethal to each other or to those around them.

Isolated from each other, Mary and Joe may be healthy. But before too long in this relationship, each will begin to manifest the relationship's symptoms. For instance, a depressed relationship will inevitably lead to a depressed Joe or a depressed Mary.

If after sensitive but thorough communication, Joe and Mary still cannot come together without a destructive effect, they may need to end their intimate relationship. The good news is they can end it armed with important knowledge that decreases the chances they will ever again become caught in a similar negative intimacy struggle.

And of course there is also the reverse. Mary and Joe may find that out of the storms of their relationship their forthright communication builds the perfect foundation for the happy intimacy each desires.

* * *

The second major source of relationship distress dwells in the partners themselves. If each person has a life script that programs him or her to respond to stress by moving into distress, the negative energy—the distress—also will be channeled into the relationship.

When newlyweds Eric and Pauline were not able to communicate their inner differences and messages, they unwittingly fed their distresses into their relationship. The relationship grew increasingly angrier and silent as their frustrated rages grew.

A few years ago, something similar happened to me. It was my misfortune to become a landlord. I can honestly say the experience was the curse of my life. I was the most forlornly accidental landlord anyone can imagine. I didn't know I was going to be one, and I never had had any intention of being one, but because of the vagaries of the United States legal system and an investment gone awry, I turned out to be one.

It seemed to me as if every moment of the day and the often-awakened night some tortured anxiety would invade my consciousness. Law suits, painters, contractors, landscapers, plumbers, vandalism, water leaks, broken sewers, floods, robberies, and other odious responsibilities of being a landlord invaded even the sanctity of my marriage bed.

"I love you," Ingrid would say as we held one another, relaxing toward sleep.

"Did John pay the rent?" I would reply, wide awake, no hope of sleep in sight.

"I said, I love you," she would say patiently.

"Yes, I know. But did he pay the rent?"

The situation was both ridiculous and terrible. I sold the apartments as quickly as I could, and only wish I could have sold them sooner. But I learned two great lessons. The first was never again to assume an expertise I didn't have. And the second was to beware of the ease and power that we, without even realizing it, can channel into our intimate relationships something that has almost an obsessively destructive quality about it.

One's work, taken home, can pipe negatively into the relationship. One's children, who must be taken home, can often pipe negatively into the relationship. Whatever our interests and cares, our responsibilities and fears, when taken home and introduced into our loving, intimate relationship with the symptoms of distress, can stifle the relationship, perhaps immobilize it, and eventually freeze it in misery.

Fortunately, this does not need to happen.

* * *

"We have one of those remarkable relationships," the man at the cocktail party told me. "For two years we've worked in different cities—me here in Santa Barbara while she was in Houston. Our careers separate us most of the month now, but we're closer than ever. We telephone every day and write notes to each other. We have two long weekends a month together. With the difference in miles, we have to make more effort. We decided our marriage was worth it."

The German poet Rainer Maria Rilke suggests we must learn to treasure the distance that is between us. Although I don't recommend that every couple live separated by thousands of miles to make their marriages work, I think my acquaintance and his wife who have chosen to accommodate themselves to the geographical demands of two busy careers have turned a potentially disastrous situation into a celebration of the importance of their marriage.

Where there is the bonding of intimacy, amazing results can happen. But what works for some couples would be impossible for others. Remember, we are all different and have different needs.

At the other extreme, in our society we tend to think intimacy and distance are incompatible. That is not so.

There must be separation and distance in any relationship, but it must be creative. In intimacy, distance is the open door. The bird may fly away, and it may return home to the intimate relationship. The open door—distance—gives freedom of choice. We choose to be together because we want to be together, not because we are afraid to be alone. A very important distinction. Too many relationships remain relationships because of fear, not because of choice. They are intimate relationships in name only.

To discover how distance and other attributes operate in primary relationships, I'm going to draw two large interlocking circles with a shaded area between. In one circle I'll write Joe's name. In the other circle I'll write Mary's. And in the shaded intersection I'll write the name of the third person in the relationship—the Jones-Smiths. The result looks something like this:

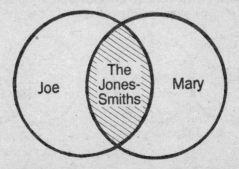

This is a very simple tool you can use to evaluate the dynamics of your marriage or primary relationship. It will help you to locate areas of strength, potential problem areas, and actual problem areas.

To show you how the circles work, we'll talk about Mary and Joe, and while we're discussing them in various situations, please be thinking about your own intimate relationship. When you're ready, draw circles for yourself and for your intimate partner. Better yet, suggest that he or she join you. This is a wonderful opportunity for two people involved in life's greatest association—intimacy—to grow through their revelations.

In our drawing, Joe has an unshaded part of one circle that is entirely his, and Mary has an unshaded part of the other circle that is entirely hers. These two areas represent the parts of life that Joe and Mary need entirely for themselves—their creative distance.

The amount of space allotted both in real life and in the drawing is a very personal and individualistic judgment, something no one can make accurately for another. The sizes of the circles and of the shaded and unshaded parts will vary from person to person, couple to couple. For this reason, you and your partner may want to make your drawings separately.

In the troubled marriage of Bill and Barbara Tinley, their individual unshaded areas would have been very large before they began counseling. During counseling, the shaded area—the third person, the Tinleys—would have grown, taken on a larger, healthier life because of the dialogs Barbara and Bill were at last having. Consequently, their outsized unshaded areas would have shrunk. This is what the change might look like:

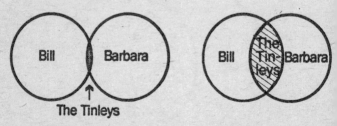

Before Counseling   **During Counseling**

Both Joe's and Mary's unshaded parts may include the word "work" because most likely neither will have much to do with the work life of the other. In another relationship, "work" or "job" might be in one partner's unshaded area, while "volunteer work," "homemaker," or something similar would be in the other's.

One of the major causes of depression in women in our particular society, especially as we climb the economic ladder, is boredom. Many wives today are victims of their husbands' successes. It isn't because Joe is cruel to Mary, and it isn't because Mary is lazy and doesn't want to do anything but spend his money and stay home and chat with her friends.

The situation is an extremely distressful application of the stress of adaptation to a life in which success has removed conflict. I treat many people who tend to be very successful in various walks of life, and I would say that this is the number one problem in dealing with the array of behavioral, physical, and emotional disorders of the Marys with whom I work.

The problem is of what to do with a successful life-style in which there is very little conflict, very little challenge, and wealthy Mary is bored out of her mind. And you know what happens when people are bored—they become boring themselves, which is of course another source of great conflict and stress.

In this situation, Mary's circle most likely would be smaller than Joe's, the amount a reflection of her smaller, more circumscribed, prisonlike life. When Mary's circle—or Joe's for that matter—is significantly smaller, then try as she might, she cannot make her contribution to the shaded area, to the nurturing of the relationship. And that presents some very, very big problems. Their relationship would look something like this:

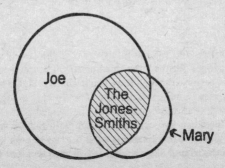

Not a very happy picture, but like many situations we create, the Marys and Joes caught in this dissatisfying life-style can change it.

Besides the word "work," Joe and Mary's unshaded circles—their lives apart—may include phrases like:

- Time alone with children

- Recreation such as golf, tennis, bowling with friends

- Business or work-related meals, conferences, and seminars

- Community work, charities, philanthropies

- Further education

- Self-improvement

- Reading and quiet contemplation

- Individual household responsibilities and chores

If Joe and Mary were in my office, I would spend considerable time asking each to fill in as completely as possible what he or she sees as needs in this area—their creative distance. I would ask them to write the phrases in the unshaded areas of their circles.

Now would be a good time for you to do this, too. Please give yourself plenty of time. Out of these lists can come many fruitful discussions with your partner. Each of us has expectations for ourselves and for our partner. With list in hand, you can begin revealing discussions about "needs," "expectations," and areas of disagreement. Remember, creative distance—as well as togetherness—is healthy and necessary for all of us.

* * *

Now let's address the intersection of the two circles, in this case the "Jones-Smiths," the third person. The intersection is very important because through it we can begin to evaluate the health of the third person in the relationship. The secret to a happy relationship is to find an intersected area—the shaded part—with which both partners can live comfortably and with fulfillment.

The shaded part represents what belongs to both partners—in other words, shared experiences. It will include areas like:

Sexual relationship
Sleep
Meals
Conversation
Recreation
Children
Hobbies

Please think about your relationship and list the areas you share with your special intimacy partner. Take as much time as you like.

* * *

When thinking about the third person in a relationship—represented by the shaded area our two circles share—we must judge not only according to size, but also according to depth.

Remember my acquaintance from the cocktail party who no longer lived full-time with his wife because of their career commitments? He said that although their situation was not optimal, it was something they chose to live with and make the most of for the time being. In their situation, their intersected shaded area—their marriage—would be small, but the shading would be dark, emphasizing the depth of their committed intimacy and of the quality of the time they were able to spend together.

Quality is very important. Mary and Joe might spend fifteen hours every day together in their marriage and quickly grow bored, thus draining their relationship of energy and damaging it. For them, perhaps three hours a day of high-quality togetherness—in which they really are attuned and together—would be the most nurturing.

Sometimes a couple's two circles will lie almost on top of each other. This usually happens during intense shared events—enjoyable events, such as taking a trip together, or profoundly disturbing events, such as sickness or the death of someone close. In these circumstances, the two persons might have very little time apart and, consequently, little distance. Necessity will strengthen their relationship, or it will weaken it, depending on many of the personality characteristics and levels of relationship that we have talked about in this book.

We learn that relationships, like life, are never static, and that fluctuations in quantity and intensity are part of the world's ebb and flow. Our circles must shift with circumstance.

And then there are vacations. At home in your regular environment, you might be very happy, in love with your intimate other, satisfied, enjoying the various aspects of your life.

And so the two of you decide to take a magnificent vacation together. You both arrange it. You anticipate it with great eagerness. But once on the vacation, once your two circles almost overlap—by choice, remember—you begin to feel suffocated. Out of the suffocation comes explosions of anger and frustration. The vacation is spoiled. And you fear that your entire life together is forever ruined.

What's happened? Dynamite has resulted from your nitrogen and your partner's glycerine. That's all. Put simply: your vacation for you was too much togetherness.

Remember, every person needs personal distance, whatever that amount may be.

When that distance evaporates, stress quickly moves in. Because of our ignorance, the stress often degenerates into distress.

That, among other reasons, is why vacations and holidays are often very busy times for psychotherapists.

Now let's take a look at the final circles of one of our Mary-and-Joe couples—a visual reflection of their relationship:

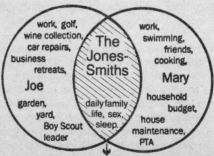

family vacations, discussions, listening to music together, going out for entertainment without children, attending children's activities, household shopping.

This Joe and Mary are busy, active people. Each has separate interests as well as many shared interests. By discussing their intersecting area—the third person in their relationship—they find themselves talking about love, the future, enjoyment, pleasure in one another, and the ongoing peace and serenity of living in a happy, committed relationship. Their third person—the Jones-Smiths—is robust with health.

If you haven't finished working on your circles, please do so now. Think carefully about the interests you've written in each section. Look at the size of your circles and at the size of the shaded area representing your relationship. Consider the depth and quality of the relationship. If you and your partner have made separate drawings, compare them.

Where are your greatest personal strengths? Your partner's greatest strengths? Your relationship's greatest strengths? Does each of you have a sense of serenity, harmony, and security about your relationship? Do you lack satisfaction? Does your partner? Where are your problem areas? Your partner's problem areas? Your relationship's problem areas?

Now is a perfect opportunity for you to talk together. Through communication, we build bridges across our rivers of fear and distress. And once across, we can journey toward our own individuation, the writing of our own life scripts, alone and together.

CHAPTER 10

REVITALIZING RELATIONSHIPS

> Man should live according to his own nature; he should con-
> centrate on self-knowledge and then live in accordance with
> the truth about himself. . . . [One] must discover one's own
> individuality, that center of personality which is equidistant
> between the conscious and the unconscious; we must aim for
> that ideal point towards which nature appears to be directing
> us. Only from that point can one satisfy one's needs.
> —C.G. JUNG
> *C.G. Jung Speaking*

"I don't want a divorce, but I don't know what else to do."

"Our relationship is special. We're attuned to one another, almost as if we're in each other's skins. I'm afraid it's too good to
be true. What can we do to make sure we don't lose it?"

"I just met this terrific man. We might actually have a chance
together. What can I do this time to make sure it lasts?"

"We've been married thirty-seven years. Most of our friends
have gotten divorces in the last five. We look at each other and
worry. What can we do to make sure divorce doesn't happen to
us?"

If intimacy is essential to the fulfillment of our humanness,
then relationship is crucial as the structure in which intimacy can
live and thrive. Just as a child grows through various stages of
development until mature relationships are possible, so intimacy
grows through very real developmental stages all the way to the
intimacy of death.

That is how necessary relationship is. Whether we are involved in a relationship that is wonderful and healthy and we pray never fails . . .

Whether we are involved in a relationship we fear is ailing . . .

Or whether we are without a relationship but yearn to have one . . .

We want to know how to grow, sustain, and if necessary revitalize intimate relationships. We want all the information we can obtain. Information, and then the understanding of what the information means, is the basis of knowledge. Without information, how can anyone make intelligent choices? Right wrongs? Forge ahead? And especially, fulfill our genetic need to create lasting, loving intimate relationships?

Some schools today are beginning to offer classes in these areas. How I wish all of us could have received thorough early education about how to form and maintain healthy, happy relationships.

According to an Associated Press report, three District of Columbia high schools recently offered eleventh graders a daily year-long class called the Dynamics of Relationships.

Why?

Because educators were concerned the youths might not be able to obtain the information they needed in their homes. More than half of the almost 90,000 students in the District of Columbia's public school system were from broken homes. Not so surprising when you think about your own adult acquaintances. The chances are excellent that about half of them have been through at least one divorce, too.

As a society, we have grown more demanding that our marriages fulfill our needs, but we are still learning how to create marriages that will do so. Until we can make those kinds of successful marriages, divorce statistics will remain high.

According to provisional figures from the National Bureau on Health Statistics, 1,159,000 couples in the United States were divorced in 1985. But since we still want intimacy, and marriage has not gone out of style, more than twice that number—2,458,000— married in the same year. One hopes that every divorced couple and every newly married couple has the information and experience to make their new relationships intimate, happy, and long-lasting, but I fear that is a forlorn hope.

An overview of the District of Columbia's high school pilot course is revealing. Its details and scope offer a microcosm of personal and relationship development that may give you some insight into the extent of your own preparation to have successful relationships:

> FORMATION: Self-esteem, what it means to be a man or a woman, friendship, dating, courtship, engagement, sexuality, marital expectations, selecting a partner, interfaith and interracial marriages, living together, and being single.
>
> MAINTENANCE: Communication, sharing, jealousy, making love work, separate but equal identities, and marriage counseling.
>
> CHANGE: Working women, housefathers, pregnancy, parenting, physical abuse, sexual abuse, drug and alcohol abuse, living with a mentally or physically ill family member, growing apart, separation, single parenting, and remarriage.
>
> TERMINATION: Divorce and its causes and consequences, loneliness, death, and dying.

If you had very little education about most of these areas when you were growing up, you're one of a vast crowd. That is the way our world dealt with intimacy—we either ignored it, or we assumed it was so natural that no one needed to think or talk about it. It's no wonder today's adults have problems with their intimate relationships.

When survival is the only issue, we humans get along very well, relying on our enormous brains to outwit the other animals in the jungle.

But when living is the issue—the real living that comes from a deep, intimate relationship in which can flourish the essence of Homo sapiens—we begin to have problems.

Brainpower isn't enough. We need the subtle tools of self-knowledge and communication.

And those subtle tools receive little attention and few obvious rewards in our society. Concerned about the problem, many medical schools now hold classes on "bedside manners" to teach their future doctors how to relate more warmly and effectively with patients. We have learned that human caring is a powerful healing agent.

For those of us who ignore or take for granted our intimacy needs, alienation and unwanted loneliness become our destiny. We're fortunate public education is trying to educate our young people about the problem so they can enter relationships with more information and thoughtfulness than we had.

Without formal educations in relating, today's adults are on our own, but our prognosis is good. Just as we have learned survival skills to make the most of our volatile, uncertain world, we also can learn living skills to enjoy the fruits of our humanness amidst all of our spectacular technology.

It takes some work, but there is laughter and illumination—as well as our old friend pain—along the way.

And so when clients come to me and ask how to begin a healthy intimate relationship, how to heal a troubled marriage or relationship, or how to sustain an already strong intimate relationship, I am pleased. Their concern is a major step forward for the development of our society's humanness, and with the appropriate work on their part, they have an excellent chance of achieving what they want.

When working with others—as well as with myself—I find the same tools that help us to revitalize our precious intimacies also help us to create and sustain them.

Interesting, isn't it?

The fertile soil in which intimacies thrive is the same fertile soil in which an ailing intimacy can be transplanted, cared for, and nurtured back to blooming health.

To create the necessary soil—that personal environment—in which your intimate relationships can flourish or become revitalized, we will talk in the next three chapters about a very simple formula I have developed. The formula calls for three ingredients essential to intimacy revitalization and good health.

The ingredients are:

- Commitment
- Priority
- Discipline

* * *

One of the questions I hear most frequently in my office is: "How do I know this marriage (or relationship) is worth saving?"

Many of the people who come to see me are emotionally bruised, psychologically exhausted, and at their wits' end. They have tried to work out their relationship problems alone or with the help of family and friends. When that fails, they seek at last professional advice.

I often hear similar questions from the audiences who attend my lectures. Earnest and concerned, these people also have troubled relationships, or they fear their relationships might become troubled.

Alas, unlike our bodies which we can X-ray, weigh, and measure in other ways, we have no quickly accurate mechanical device to evaluate the health of our relationships.

Instead, we must rely on our humanness for our answers—the very humanness that is often both cause and cure of the trouble in our relationships.

Intimacy has difficult-to-measure, often intangible criteria. In intimacy, we channel our individual essence through the craft of relating. The result is a constant flow of our innermost humanness through the skills we are talking about in this book. The criteria of intimacy can be judged only by those involved in the relationship, sometimes aided by the trained viewer, seldom by technology.

And so this is the answer I give: "It's a feeling."

Feelings are our own very human, very personalized measuring systems for what is right and wrong in our lives.

Most people know gut level, deep down, whether there is anything left in their relationship. If they feel there is, I encourage them to try to revitalize the relationship.

If they feel there is not—and are not in a counseling situation —I suggest they consult a professional because, when we are in a relationship that is ailing, we find being objective extremely difficult, often impossible. And so sometimes a person needs an outside evaluation from a referee, from somebody who is not emotionally involved, somebody who is trained to look at diagnostic factors such as sex life, communication, commitment, and attitudes. Information from an outside professional often clarifies muddy situations so we can make the decision best for us.

If we decide that there is even a remote flicker of life in our relationship, then we can know the relationship is worth fighting for.

And then, as we do the work, how do we know that the revitalizing is taking effect?

Again, it's a feeling. It's as if you've been ill for a very long time, an invalid, and now you're mending, feeling stronger and better little by little every day. People often explain it to me this way:

"We're just able to talk about more things than we were able to before."

"We're beginning to enjoy each other again."

"Now we're actively looking for things we can do together."

The more you realize the relationship is improving, the more risks you begin to take, and then comes the wonderful discovery that the relationship can support those risks. You, your partner, and your relationship are not only mending; like fresh new grass you're growing again.

* * *

How do we accomplish the birth, maintenance, and revitalizing of intimacy?

There's no secret involved.

Remember, we have a genetic drive for intimacy, and we have a built-in ability to adapt.

And now by reading this book you are gathering information that will help you to put to use your adaptability so your intimacy needs can be fulfilled.

In this book we have explored the primary causes of our fears of intimacy—fear of abandonment, success, and rejection.

We have also investigated the causes of burnout and distress in intimate relationships—ignoring our stresses, those neutral, internal calls for change.

We have seen how fear and distress cooperate in destroying our relationships. And we have seen that we can challenge our fears and use stress as a transformational tool to achieve intimacy.

Now it's time to develop new attitudes that we can apply to our relationships.

With *commitment, priority,* and *discipline,* we can:

Impose our natural strengths over our old scripts of fear, distress, and misery

Gain more control over our lives and how we want to shape them

Make changing easier, pleasanter, and more understandable.

And with the knowing application of these three attitudes, each of us can become the kind of person who can create the loving, lasting relationship that will transform our lives.

CHAPTER 11

COMMITMENT—COUNTERPOINT TO CRISIS

> Every man carries within him the eternal image of woman, not the image of this or that particular woman, but a definite female image. This image is fundamentally unconscious. The same is true of the woman: she too has her inborn image of man. . . . Since this image is unconscious, it is always unconsciously projected upon the person of the beloved, and is one of the chief reasons for passionate attraction or aversion.
>
> —C.G. JUNG
> *Marriage as a Psychological Relationship*

A few years ago my eighty-five-year-old mother, who lives in England, decided to visit us. She'd never been to the United States. I'd been trying to persuade my parents to come for some time. Then my father died, and my mother was alone. At last she agreed to make the trip.

After looking around our back yard, Ingrid decided that building a terraced flower garden would be really nice to do before my mother arrived. We already had a fish pond with a little water fountain. Ingrid wanted to serve my mother breakfast every morning next to the fish pond, and—with a view of our beautiful new flower garden—my mother would have a very pleasant beginning to each of her days with us.

As you can see, Ingrid is a loving and thoughtful person. And although she is also a very busy businesswoman, she wanted to do this for my mother. She began to make arrangements.

Then one evening I drove home late from my counseling clinic. It was nine o'clock, and I'd been working since seven that morning. You know that wonderful feeling when you've had a long day, you're very tired, and you swing into your own driveway. At that point you can finally relax. You're home safe. You let your eyelids droop, put yourself on automatic pilot, punch the garage door opener, and expect to come to a restful stop in your own garage.

Instead I found my car going straight up an enormous mountain of dirt.

Two tons of soil for the future garden had been deposited in our driveway a full week before it was needed. It filled the driveway and blocked the garage door. We hadn't even picked up the railroad ties yet, which we needed to build the terraces before the dirt was shoveled in, but somehow Ingrid hadn't understood how much space was required to store two tons of dirt. She'd ordered the planting soil too early.

I stared at that mountain of dirt, my hands on the steering wheel, my front wheels up off the pavement. I could have ruined the front end of my car.

My shock was wearing off. I was getting very angry.

Too big to move, the dirt pile would have to remain where it was all week. If it rained, we'd have a big, muddy mess on our hands. Also, there were problems associated with not being able to get into the garage. And I could just see us trying to carry the railroad ties into the yard around that vast mountain.

The more I thought about the situation, the more furious I grew.

Just then Stewart, our Rhodesian Ridgeback dog, came bounding out of the house to greet me. He and I decided to take a little walk; I knew I needed to think things out. I backed the car off the mountain of earth, turned off the motor, and away we went.

There was a time when I wouldn't have taken the walk. I would have rushed into the house, furious, self-righteous. The old me would have been very, very cutting to Ingrid, using all my verbal skills to slash and decimate her with sharp words and a biting tone of voice. I would have been so caught up in my own anger and outrage that—without necessarily realizing it—my goal would have been to punish her instead of resolving the problem.

Instead, Stewart and I walked.

Ingrid and I had been married only a few months then. I wanted very much for our relationship to continue to flourish. Fortunately, I had learned a few things from past mistakes. I began to think about the present situation.

As my anger cooled, I realized this was the woman with whom I'd be going to bed that night.

This was the woman with whom, God willing, in the morning I would awaken.

This was the woman with whom I wanted to share all of the joys and sadnesses of life—and this would be going on for as long as we both were alive.

And then I realized that Ingrid was the woman in whose arms I would die one day, or in my arms she would die if she were to go first.

She was the woman with whom I had made the commitment of my life in a way I'd never made a commitment before. I meant this commitment. If I failed to sustain my marvelous relationship with her, I didn't know where else I could go because I couldn't make any stronger commitment than I'd made with Ingrid.

Was I going to risk injuring my relationship with Ingrid over a pile of dirt?

The situation became absurd. Of course I wouldn't. I couldn't.

Instead of following my old destructive pattern of making some very deep, bone-level verbal wounds, I needed to find a new way to communicate with this woman who meant so much to me.

Stewart and I headed for home, armed with a fresh and very personal understanding of commitment.

I went into the house. Ingrid was waiting, apprehensive, worried. She did not know how I would react to the mistake.

I put my hands on her shoulders. I was still angry, and in times of anger touching is important. I said to her, "You know, there are three things I want to tell you. First, if I hadn't already asked you to marry me, I would now because I love you very much. Second, you screwed up the arrangements for the garden very badly, which has made me angry. And third, may I help by calling a landscaping company tomorrow? We'll have them come in and do the whole thing. Then you and I can plant the flowers so the garden will be ours together. That way there won't be any unresolved bitterness and anger between us."

That is what happened. The landscapers came, and then Ingrid and I planted a beautiful garden. When my mother visited, she sat beside the pond each morning and enjoyed the flowers my wife and I had planted in love.

From this incident I learned a great lesson, and Ingrid understood my need to relearn what is important in life.

* * *

Why did I tell you this story? For several reasons. One is that each of us is angered and frustrated by different situations. What was a 9 on my stress scale may be only a 2 on yours. But my 9 was very real and dangerous for me, just as your 9s are very real and dangerous for you. The important link between your 9s and my 9s is perspective.

Another reason was to show you that commitment can give perspective against which to measure the importance of outrage and anger. A deep commitment to the primary person in your life can give you the perspective to heal and grow your relationship:

The level of your commitment is a counterpoint to the crises in your intimate relationship.

What would it take to break up your relationship? If your commitment and your partner's commitment are total, then nothing would.

But if your commitment or your partner's commitment is relative, then you have to start asking yourself, "Okay, what *would* break us up?"

- If she cheats on me . . .

- If he drinks too much . . .

- If she doesn't quit spending so much money . . .

- If he doesn't find a job . . .

If one of those situations were to happen to you, what would you do?

A relative commitment will break under the pressure of certain external crises. In intimacy therapy, the level of commitment is a significant measure of the health of the relationship, and an area where important, honest work can be accomplished.

Now would be a good time for you and your partner to examine your commitment to each other and to your relationship. Be as ruthless as possible. Apply our usual 10-point scale, 1 being low, and 10 being high.

Is your commitment a 1, a 5, or a 10? Please spend some time thinking about how deep your commitment is.

* * *

Commitment, of course, is the bonding of the Jones-Smiths.

We saw much of that reflected in the image of the shaded area where their two circles intersected. As the two circles move outwards and the shaded area gets smaller and smaller, then the value level of the commitment drops. As the commitment decreases, smaller and smaller crises can destroy this intersection.

Without commitment, there is no counterpoint to crisis, which is why in so many relationships relatively trivial events inflate into relationship-destroying explosions. We pile wound upon mortal wound, often without knowing what we are doing to the other, and not truly aware of what the other is doing to us. At the end, both good people wonder what on earth happened to them.

Many of us have had experiences in which something trivial—some word, some gesture, some look, some event, some accident or forgetfulness—has been inflated by the other person into a major relationship crisis. And after the explosion, if our awestruck gaze is clear, in the midst of the debris we can see a relationship that is dying. The commitment must be to the life of the relationship, not to its death.

The greater the degree of commitment, the larger the crisis that can be overcome. A 100 percent commitment shelters us against a 100 percent crisis. A 50 percent commitment offers no shelter against a 75 percent crisis, and life is full of 75 percent crises.

- With a 50 percent commitment, I'll stay with you if you get sick, unless of course you become a vegetable. Then you wouldn't expect me to stay on, would you? With a 100 percent commitment, I'd say yes.

- With a 50 percent commitment, if you had an affair with someone, you wouldn't expect me to swallow that, would you? With a 100 percent commitment, I'd say yes. It would hurt. It would devastate me. It would sure make me wonder why you had to do that. It would make me ask for what changes reality was calling. I apparently wasn't listening to that call, and that caused you to do something that was probably a scream for help. I didn't hear the scream then, but I hear it now and, yes, I forgive you and, yes, if this can be worked out we will work it out—together.

* * *

Earlier in this book you made an evaluation of the levels of the stresses and distresses in your life. Now you have examined your commitment level. A comparison of the numbers may be enlightening for you.

Even if the stresses in your life are fairly low level, you will occasionally have 9s and 10s explode around you. Some people live at a constant level of 8s, 9s, and 10s. Others live in the middle level at the 4s, 5s, and 6s. And then there are the few who live blissfully with low-level stress, ranging from 1s to 4s.

Please look at the numbers you've attached to your stresses.

Are most of those numbers higher than the number you gave to your level of commitment?

Are they higher than the number that your partner rates his or her commitment?

If most of your stress ratings are higher, you have a very good indication of serious problems in your relationship. But with that information, you also have causes, areas for fruitful discussion with your partner, and—I hope you've learned in this book—tools to begin resolving your problems.

However, if your stress numbers are honestly lower than your commitment numbers, you will find you and your partner have developed skills to deal with and overcome crises and stresses.

You already may have the kind of intimacy most meaningful to you.

* * *

In some instances, marriages can be the ugliest, most warped relationships on earth. There's a lot of emotional abuse in some marriages. There's a lot of rape in some marriages. There's a lot of violence in some marriages. Unfortunately, some marriages are not worth the parchment on which they're recorded.

The possession of a wedding certificate does not instantly transform a relationship into something ethereal.

But still, in our society marriage is our ancient symbol for officially acknowledging our total commitment to our intimate relationship. With it, there are no ifs and buts. Good or bad, you'll find no easy way out of marriage.

The wedding vows—whether made in a church, tabernacle, mosque, home, or courthouse—give us an opportunity to examine the meaning of commitment. A 100 percent commitment is frightening for many of us:

- Who can swear to that kind of commitment with certainty?

- Who can foresee all the future circumstances that will work against our being able to keep it?

- How do we know that we will be able—much less want—to stay together through joy and disaster, wealth or poverty, illness and health, forsaking all others until death us do part?

The answer is that we don't know. And that we don't need to know. Total commitment is perhaps the greatest risk any human can make.

It must be made without foreknowledge of the future. It expresses your love of and vulnerability to the primary person in your life. It expresses the value you place on the relationship.

And it expresses your willingness to risk your love, time, effort, and honor.

The total commitment is to life with all its changes. A marriage is not just a sheet of paper. It's a living entity.

It's the third person in the relationship.

As we find joy and excitement in one another, the third person blossoms with happiness. As we learn to solve our problems together, the third person grows more intelligent and confident. As we face life's tragedies and embrace each other in grief, the third person grows stronger, more compassionate, and more resilient. As we grow wiser with life, the third person grows wiser, too.

Your commitment can be the vehicle for your freedom.

Contrary to popular belief, marriage and your marriage partner are not a "ball and chain." When we enter marriage, we do not enter prison. Instead we are offered opportunities to liberate ourselves. As Abraham Maslow says so well in *Toward a Psychology of Being*, ". . . [human] growth customarily takes place in little steps, and each step forward is made possible by the feeling of being safe, of operating out into the unknown from a safe home port, of daring because retreat is possible."

A vital intimate marriage is the safest, most nurturing home port.

No matter how brave, tough, or strong we are, each of us needs this kind of base. Without it, we wander the universe only partially fulfilled. But with it, we can challenge the stars and achieve the kinds of successes that are important to us. We also can make new kinds of friendships with members of the opposite sex— honest relationships based on liking and respect, not tainted by sexual gameplaying that leads to bed as a substitute for communication.

Commitment means freedom.

With total commitment by both you and your partner, you can be who you are without fear. You can do what is best without reprisal. You can love with safety. And you can be loved with complete knowledge that your partner knows who you are—the good and the bad—and loves you the more for it.

* * *

On watching a space launch:

There was flame. There was fire. The ground trembled as the enormous rocket rose through the murky smoke into the bright morning sky. On its back the rocket carried a small silver space ship.

At last the space ship separated from the big rocket. It flew off, far from the turbulence of the rocket's propulsion.

The space ship was in orbit. All was well. The blast-off was only the means to an end.

The rocket tumbled back to earth, the tasks of its engines completed.

But the space ship soared on into the heavens, its long life just beginning.

Falling in love is like a space launch, full of flame and fire, full of the energy necessary to reach the next stage of the relationship.

Going into orbit requires a different energy. If the couple's desire to orbit—to commit to an intimate relationship—isn't achieved by the time the rocket burns out of fuel, then the launch can no longer sustain its fiery thrust. The mission has to be aborted. Both the rocket and the ship of the relationship tumble away back to earth, crash.

Some people can sustain only the blast-off—the falling in love —which is the preliminary stage of a relationship. For them, relationships turn out to be perpetual launchings and tumblings away, never quite reaching the orbit of intimacy.

Those of us in this situation have one honeymoon after another with one partner after another. Slowly we grow dissatisfied, unhappy. Eventually we yearn to soar on into intimacy, but we don't know how, we are afraid, and often we are suspicious. Sometimes we withdraw, avoid having relationships of any kind with potential partners. Other times we keep on with our honeymoons, with which at least we've learned to have a degree of success.

Remember the fears we talked about—fear of success, abandonment, and rejection? These fears can keep us from getting what we need and want from life.

Getting married in the fire and flame of the blast-off stage of the relationship is extremely dangerous.

The best time to make a commitment and to marry is when the ship of the relationship is ready to go into orbit.

But how does a person know he or she wants to marry—wants and is ready to totally commit to an intimate relationship?

A friend who liked my rocket-and-spaceship analogy explained it this way:

> I was separated and then divorced seven years, and during that period I dated many wonderful women. Then I met Helen. It seemed what I was searching for I had found in her—the love, excitement, passion, kindness, intelligence—so many qualities I can't even begin to name them all.
>
> Helen and I reached a point where the excitement was still at a high pitch, but that we were somehow looking around, maybe waiting for something to happen. Then little things about each other began to annoy us for no reason we could see.
>
> We began to realize our relationship would end soon in the blast-off stage, as so many before had ended for each of us. Our rocket was out of fuel for sustaining the status quo. We had gone as far as we could with our relationship the way it was.
>
> But Helen and I looked at each other and knew we didn't want to lose each other. As we talked, we saw that for us to continue, we needed a different kind of relationship.
>
> The next stage was commitment. And so I asked myself, "Why wouldn't I marry Helen?" I realized I was tired of searching. I didn't want to put more fuel into blast-offs. The constant honeymoons didn't make me happy anymore. There was something missing from my life.
>
> We both wanted our relationship to grow into whatever it could be.
>
> It was time to gamble. I was scared. We were both scared.

We didn't know if we could make a marriage work. But we couldn't go back to our endless, repetitive honeymoons either.

So we made the commitment of marriage, trusting that we would work problems out as they came up. When we decided to forge ahead, I had a sense of accomplishment. It seemed to me as though my war was at last over.

For us, it's been one step at a time. We've laughed a lot, and we've made a lot of mistakes.

We're each other's only lovers, and we're also best friends. I like the specialness of marriage, of knowing how special I am to Helen, and of getting that catch in my throat when I think about how special she is to me.

When you know this is it for life, a real commitment—well, you realize you have to make it work. It's your responsibility. No one can do it for you. You start to get proud of that.

And you're grateful, too. You know if you go broke, get Alzheimer's disease—whatever the disaster—you'll weather it together.

Abandoning Helen is unthinkable. With Helen, colors are brighter, days are sunnier, life is full of opportunities. I couldn't love her this much if I hadn't made the commitment.

We've been married ten years now, and I thank God for every single day.

CHAPTER 12

PRIORITY—TIME, ENERGY, AND MONEY

As is well known, one understands nothing psychological unless one has experienced it oneself. Not that this ever prevents anyone from feeling convinced that his own judgment is the only true and competent one.

—C.G. JUNG
Marriage as a Psychological Relationship

Many of us are singularly unaware of who we really are. We are aware of who we're supposed to be, and we feel terribly guilty because we never seem able to achieve that pinnacle. Just imagine what would happen if you were to replace who you are "supposed" to be with the acceptance of who you are.

Suddenly you would measure up.

No longer would you have the oughts, the shoulds, the musts, the shouldn'ts, and the oughtn'ts of other people to live up to.

"You should lose ten pounds. You'd look and feel much better."

"You should *gain* ten pounds. You'd look and feel much better."

"A person with your education ought to be earning much more money."

"As boys and girls grow up, boys get smarter and girls get dumber. That's the way it's supposed to be."

"You oughtn't to disappoint your parents like that. Look what they've sacrificed for you."

Guilt and fear keep many of us tied to others' expectations for us. Increasingly we measure our self-worth by others' ideas of perfection.

Whether from society at large, our parents, or our friends, the standards we try to achieve are too often wrong, worthless, and impossible for us. The goals and standards may be too high, too low, or simply inappropriate. Pursuing them makes us deeply unhappy.

We can decide to leave this behind. Instead we can embark on perhaps the most important journey of our lives. We can discover ourselves.

Who are you really? What do you really want out of life?

You may have no inkling. Or your answers may be fuzzy. Or by answering the questions you may find you are curious to know more about yourself. Whatever your reason, once you begin the study of yourself and who you really are, your basic personality— the real you—gradually will unfold and reveal itself.

As you go through life in this more realistic condition, you are no longer at the mercy of others' needs, fears, and unfulfilled dreams.

You cannot fail because you will always meet your own newly scripted expectations. You need have no guilt because you at last measure up.

With a healthy set of ethics, life becomes a series of successes that are admirable, significant, and fulfilling to the most important person in the world—*you*.

Consider my plight with the mountain of dirt in my driveway. When faced with similar situations in the past, I'd acted stupidly. I'd hurt others, and by doing that I'd hurt myself. I'd also kept myself from getting completely what I most needed and wanted— intimacy.

There were many complicated reasons for my behavior, but at the foundation was that I was living not only my life, but others' lives as well. Just as we've been discussing, I was trying to fulfill other people's expectations for me. At one time or another, most of us do this, too many of us sentencing ourselves to lifetimes of it.

Such excesses sound idiotic, don't they? Nevertheless, they are common in human behavior.

Some of us eventually see the inappropriate behavior in others.

That helps us to see it in ourselves.

And once we recognize what we're doing to ourselves, we can begin to move beyond and into lives right and honorable for each individual one of us.

By the time of my marriage to Ingrid, my self-knowledge had grown enough that I often knew when I was replaying old, destructive scripts. That recognition was crystallized by my commitment to Ingrid and to our relationship.

Without commitment, a relationship cannot get into orbit. But with commitment coupled with enlightened self-knowledge, we can begin to form the nurturing soil in which we can grow, maintain, and heal the relationships that each of us needs.

Commitment is the first step.

Priority is the second step.

Without placing our intimate relationships high on our lists of priorities, our commitments mean nothing. Our commitments become empty words that will not stand up to the test of crisis.

Many of us are uncomfortable placing our relationship commitments high in our priorities. We are afraid, and we hide our fear behind such ideas as:

"If we really love each other, commitment isn't necessary."

"I don't believe in commitment."

"There's no point in making a commitment. Our relationship probably won't last anyway."

"Of course I made a commitment. We got married, didn't we?"

A person with a fear of commitment may be precisely another version of a person with a fear of rejection. Often the common denominator in both of these anxieties is an abandonment neurosis.

Remember Charlie's testing? His unconscious goal was to test his relationships beyond their abilities to endure. When at last his women left, he could say with honesty and relief, "I always knew she'd abandon me."

Unfortunately, many people manipulate relationships so that

they make no real commitment. In this way they avoid being abandoned by doing the abandoning themselves.

Does any of this sound familiar in your life or in the lives of those around you?

These common manipulations are very distressful and potentially lethal methods of dealing with fears of abandonment. They are self-fulfilling. *If I fix things so that you abandon me or I can claim good cause to abandon you, then I have strengthened my conviction that I am essentially unlovable and that, despite my best efforts, I must spend my life alone.* Do you see the controlling "must" of this expectation?

Here is where self-knowledge can play a vital role. Somewhere in the past someone's expectations for us were wrong. Those of us with abandonment neuroses accepted the message that we were so unlovable that we couldn't count on anyone's staying with us. Then we set about fulfilling that unhappy prophecy in our intimate relationships.

When this happens, other people's expectations have taken us over, telling us which priorities to have.

But once we begin the study of who we really are, we also begin to free ourselves from these inappropriate expectations.

At last we can make our own priorities.

With a sincere commitment to an intimate relationship, and with a strong desire to rank the commitment at the top of our priorities, we are firmly on the path toward creating the intimacies we desire.

* * *

How do I know where I've prioritized my intimate relationship? How do I go about raising it to the top of my priorities?

Not surprisingly, most of us are unaware of how we rank our intimate relationships. To help you discover your relationship's priority, we'll investigate three primary areas crucial to the well-being of intimacy. They are:

- Time
- Energy
- Money

As you read about each, please think about how your own life is structured. Have you chosen what is most important to you?

TIME

Most of us who are busy and successful have a real problem with time. Time is a priority over which control is very difficult to achieve. One of the penalties of success is ongoing commitment. The more successful we become at whatever we do, the more that that success generates work and responsibility, and the more that the work and responsibility demand our time.

We cannot buy time. We cannot easily delegate time. And whatever connections we may have, we're not going to pack any more than twenty-four hours into each day.

In our prioritizing of quantity of time, many of us would have to list our work as number one. If that's what you want, then that's fine for you. But if that isn't what you want, then you're living in a very stressful situation. In this case, you would have two opposing factors generating extremely negative energy. The unhappy result would be that ultimately both your work and your intimate relationship will suffer. To resolve this problem, you can either reconcile yourself to this situation, or you can make some changes.

To live a life suited to your individual needs, do some inward searching.

Establish a hierarchy of your personal priorities.

Be honest about it with those closest to you.

There's nothing wrong with an intimate relationship being a second priority in your life, provided that that's what you want, provided that it's clearly identified as such, and provided that the highest quality of life can go into making your number two priority —your intimate relationship—the best number two it can possibly be.

What is not fine is saying that your relationship is the number one priority while your intentions are that your work is number one. What happens as a result is that little quality goes into the loser in the competition, which should never be a competition in the first place. There is nothing incompatible between a first-class relationship and a first-class work situation. But there is a great deal wrong when one of them through default becomes second rate. This orphan is usually the relationship.

Most of us sleep about seven hours a day. Most of us are gone to work for eight to eleven hours. Most of us have to commute to our work. Most of us have private needs to fulfill—showers to take, going to the bathroom, and so forth.

Once you add up all those nondiscretionary hours, you're probably left—if you're very lucky—with about five hours a day of discretionary time.

How you choose to use your discretionary time tells you a lot about what priority you place on your intimate relationship.

Do you find other things to do so that you spend as little time as possible with your intimate partner? Or do you make time so that you can be together as often as possible?

And consider quality of time. You can spend all five hours of your discretionary time with your intimate partner and have the most awful, boring time imaginable. Or you can spend one hour of discretionary time together and have such a scintillating, renovating, and refreshing experience that you yearn for more and more.

If you're both sullenly reading newspapers on opposite sides of the room, if your only shared activity is watching television, you're not really together. But if you're involved in a meaningful conversation with one another in which each is actually looking into the other's eyes, hearing the other's words, and basking in the presence of the other, then your quality of time together is very high.

To grow, maintain, and heal, your intimate relationship's environment needs to be enriched by a number one commitment of quality—not necessarily quantity—of your time.

Let your marriage or relationship be the first served from the table of quality time, not the recipient of the scraps left over after all other commitments have been fed.

ENERGY

All work requires energy. All relationships require energy. Living in general requires energy. Each of us has only a certain amount of energy. It is not an unlimited resource.

Remember our discussion of stress, that it is neutral energy waiting for you to use it? Think about the energy that you perceive in your primary relationship.

Is your relationship mostly full of negative energy?

Or is your relationship mostly full of positive energy?

With negative energy, you may feel very alone in your intimate relationship. There are moments when you connect with your partner, and these give you soaring feelings of hope, or perhaps discouragement. Talking with your partner requires a lot of effort. There doesn't seem much to say. When you walk into a crowded room, you sometimes wonder why you aren't with one of the other men (or women) there. It seems as if you fight all the time with your partner. Or you seldom fight, but then you seldom talk either. Your home has holes in walls or doors where rages have driven one of you to smash your fists or feet. You complain about your partner and your relationship (or you can't understand why your partner continually complains about you and your relationship). You feel dragged out, tired, or irritable when you're together. You can't wait to get away.

On the other hand, with positive energy, laughter and happiness are a normal part of your day-to-day intimate relationship. You glow with good feelings when you are with your partner. In a crowded room, you seek each other out. You have learned to resolve your differences, problems, fears, and angers, and then go on living and loving. You can forgive each other and yourself. You care more what your partner thinks than what other people think. You are proud to go out with your partner. Life without your partner would be empty and lonely.

If you and your partner react to stress by avoiding or resisting necessary changes, the energy you pour into your relationship will be negative distressful energy.

If you and your partner react to stress by making necessary

changes, no matter how painful, the energy you pour into your relationship will be positive, transformational energy.

As we discussed in earlier chapters, stress can be rechanneled from the destructive symptoms of distress into the transformational power of de-stress. But for you to do this, you must first recognize that distress is sickening your intimate relationship.

A good question to ask yourself is whether your marriage or relationship is worth the effort it seems to require.

If your answer is no, then you know your relationship is in serious trouble.

If your answer is yes, then you can know there is a lot that is healthy about your intimacy.

The quality of energy that you and your partner are willing to give to your intimate relationship largely determines the quality of energy each of you gets back.

As with any living entity, a relationship thrives with the energy of loving attention. And if your relationship thrives, you will, too.

MONEY

Money is where you put your feet instead of just your mouth. I have known some wonderful commitments and I have known some wonderful priorities of time and energy, but I have also seen them rendered useless when it came time to pay the bill.

Why is money a priority? Because in our society money symbolizes security. In dream analysis, for instance, if a client describes a dream involving money, a therapist generally looks at that money as a symbol of security. By the way, I'm not criticizing money as a security symbol. It just happens to be one in our society.

We work for money. In a sense we evaluate a person's worth by money. We'll say, "What's he (or she) worth?" We evaluate the worthwhileness of many jobs by how much they pay.

Since money is highly symbolic in our society, we might as well incorporate that symbolism transformationally into the relationship rather than have it become a distressful symptom.

Money is one of the most frequent causes of communication breakdowns in intimate relationships.

In one scenario, the man might say, "I go out and work all day, and my wife does nothing but take care of the house and lie around, and she thinks she can go out and spend up to the hilt the money I work so hard earning in that rat race out there."

In response, the woman might say, "There's no way he could do that if I weren't keeping the home fires burning, giving him a nurturing place to which he can return for rest and refreshment so he can go back into the big world to earn his hefty salary he's so proud of."

This scenario provides a potentially explosive confrontation between two entirely different concepts of the symbolic value of money, and the power and control money gives. By the way, the male and female roles easily could be reversed here, but the unfortunate results are the same.

The major wage earner may say, "If I earn it, I have control over it, right?" To which I must reply, "Not in the sort of deeply intimate, satisfying relationship we're defining in this book."

There is another way to view this situation. One partner may work a lifetime in various jobs that give tremendous personal satisfaction. Such people identify themselves by their work. Their work is their number one priority, and the fruit of their work is not only satisfaction, but—highly important as evidence of their success to them personally—is the money they've earned.

The other partner may place his or her values in a different coin of the realm. Such people identify themselves also by their work, but their work is loving and nurturing others, and there is little financial compensation for what they do. For them, most important is kissing a tearful child's scratched finger, preparing wholesome meals, spending hours listening to the troubles and dreams of their partner or child, and perhaps donating help to less fortunate people in the community. They have little money to prove their worth; they have only intangibles which are valuable in and of themselves.

If one of these two people offers all the fruits of what he or she most values and the other does not, an imbalanced relationship results. A truly intimate relationship can take place only between equals.

If one partner holds back, the partners are not equal, the third person in the relationship is crippled, and the relationship's life expectancy is consequently shortened.

The person who offers everything while the other does not feels rejected, often accompanied by a strong sense of injustice. These wounds can cut to the bone, growing deeper and more painful with the unresolved years.

Please think about your own intimate relationship. Whose name goes on which bank accounts? Which investments? Why?

I list money as an important priority not because I personally overload money with value, but because in my work with breaking and broken relationships, money almost always is a factor. It is usually a result of serious deficiencies in communication styles and priorities.

I'd like to tell you about something simple Ingrid and I do that is important to both of us. Like you, we're both busy. And like you, our days from about eight in the morning until seven or eight at night are tightly scheduled. We have very little time and energy left unless we're willing to pay for it.

Once a week we take a two-hour lunch so we can eat leisurely together and enjoy one another's company. We talk, explore ideas, laugh, and renew ourselves in each other. This, among other simple rituals guaranteeing time together, is important to us and to our relationship.

But these little two-hour lunches also cost Ingrid and me a fair amount of money, just as they would cost you. The lunches themselves require a moderate sum, but we pay a great deal more in lost earning time. When I'm not working with clients, I'm not earning any fees. When Ingrid is eating with me, she has to pay someone to watch her store.

If you're having lunch with your wife or husband, you're not working in the office or factory. If you're not working and you're an hourly employee or a professional, you're not going to get paid. If you're in management, then you know time is money, and promotions are delayed for those whose time and energy use are not cost effective.

If your intimate partner works outside the home, she or he is probably not going to be paid either. You may be losing two incomes. And if you take a vacation together, think how much that will cost you in out-of-pocket expenses as well as lost earning time and perhaps missed business opportunities. By the way, both you and your partner may have misgivings about the cost of your relationship.

As you can see, intimate relationships can become very expensive in a number of ways.

This is what priority is all about:

Everything you want in life has a cost. If you want something, have the courage to pay for it.

In the case of your intimate relationship, if the cost is too high, then your money is more important to you than the relationship. You need to know that so you can be honest with yourself and your partner.

On the other hand, if you believe your intimate relationship is priceless, then no bank account is large enough to buy what you already possess. Money doesn't prove you to be a worthwhile human being. Money doesn't establish your independence, maturity, or responsibility.

Your money and your partner's money are not weapons to be used to keep the other greedy one at bay.

Instead your united money becomes a vehicle for your mutual sustenance, enrichment, enjoyment, and a symbol that each of you is freely and completely giving everything you have to the well-being of your most important relationship.

* * *

Now is a good time for you to examine your priorities. Try to establish which priorities are yours, and which you've inherited.

Making a list might be very helpful here. Your list would probably include quantity and quality of time, energy, and money.

Next choose which priorities you'd like to discard, and which you'd like to keep.

To achieve what you really want from life, how would you like to arrange your priorities? Make a new list reflecting your true desires.

In life, you generally get what you give. If you give everything you internally and externally possess to your beloved partner and the relationship you share, and your partner gives in kind, you will have time to enjoy one another, endless energy that you reap from your togetherness, and riches beyond any worldly expectation.

*   *   *

Question: Our cultural message often is that the success of a relationship depends mainly on the woman. How do you convince your intimate partner or husband—who believes this—to actively share in the relationship? What is the prognosis for this kind of relationship?

This is a question of priorities, and what happens when one partner's priorities are radically different from the other partner's.

In some relationships, the man's priorities make him the nonparticipant; in other relationships, the woman's priorities make her the nonparticipant. The person who has bowed out—for whatever reasons—usually expects the other partner to pick up the major responsibility for taking care of the relationship.

In either case, the results are the same—the third person in the relationship is greatly weakened, will be able to withstand very little stress, and can be expected to quickly slip into symptoms of deep distress.

In a relationship, commitment and priorities have to be equal between the partners, not in terms of volume—we're not talking about a pound of commitment each—but in terms of the capacity of each person.

Your partner's capacity for commitment and priority may be

greater than yours right now. But if your levels are up to the maximum of what you're capable, the balance is equal.

In two years, your commitment and priority capacity may be greater than your partner's, and in five years your partner's may have caught up and exceeded yours, and so forth.

In an organic relationship, there is an ebb and flow of increasing unity as we grow closer to the total commitment and high priority of which all of us are capable and which will provide us the greatest fulfillment.

When your commitment or arrangement of priorities depends upon cultural norms or upon the expectations of other people, or when your partner's does, then the third person of your relationship will quickly ail and fall prey to most stresses.

How do you convince your partner to share actively in your relationship?

Such a relationship predictably will have problems because of the inequality of participation. The problems may range from choice of living locations to child care and outside relationships. The person who is the nonparticipant should not be shielded from the problems, their consequences, and the resulting relationship distresses.

Confrontation rather than acquiescence is usually the most effective means of compelling the nonparticipant to face the problems.

The partner who is reluctant to confront the nonparticipant is practicing a refined form of cowardice. The ship is sinking, but this person doesn't want to risk the disturbance caused by sounding the alarm.

On the other hand, the nonparticipant doesn't want the alarm sounded either. Sometimes a nonparticipant will call me on the telephone and say, "Doctor, I'm going to send my wife (or husband) in to see you because she (he) really needs help. I've heard good things about you, that you've fixed up other people. Maybe you can do the same for my wife (husband)."

Sigmund Freud had a reply for this situation. He'd say, "Keep the person who does the bringing, and send home the one who is brought."

Unless the partners begin meaningful dialogue, the prognosis for this relationship is emotional torpor. The relationship will continue one-sided and grow more and more hideously boring and nonnurturing, perhaps at last becoming toxic.

The couple might look great in the country club, but awful in the intimacy of their own home.

Meanwhile, the partner on whose shoulders rests the responsibility for the relationship will grow as weak as the third person in the relationship. This partner is in danger of cracking up. Eventually if no changes occur, the issue may be simply who cracks up first—the partner or the relationship.

But there is another potential result to this grim situation. Instead of the inevitable death of the relationship, this opportunity could lead to a transformed, uniquely fulfilling relationship.

Remember our discussion of stresses, that the 10s offered not only the greatest possibility of life-threatening devastation but also the greatest possibility of life-giving transformation?

This is one of those situations.

Here the partners themselves determine what happens to their relationship.

They can continue as they are, knowing that torpor and eventually relationship death will set in, or they can go to work, learn about themselves and each other and what they need individually and together. The act of self-learning—of informing themselves about themselves—is the first and most difficult step for most people.

Again the answer returns to one of choice.

Once we know more about who we really are, and once we can make our own commitments and set our own priorities, we can make the choices that are right for us.

And if we decide to revitalize and transform our existing relationships, or to end the relationships and look for more appropriate ones, we can get on with it. Just as we humans learned to control fire and harness mighty rivers, we can learn to create and sustain the intimate relationships that we individually need.

CHAPTER 13

DISCIPLINE—TECHNIQUES FOR CONTROL

The unrelated human being lacks wholeness, for he can achieve wholeness only through the soul, and the soul cannot exist without its other side, which is always found in a 'you.'
—C.G. JUNG
The Practice of Psychotherapy

"I love him," my new client told me, "and he loves me. We thought we had something special, but now we're falling apart."

Discipline is what makes our commitments and priorities work. Without discipline, love is set adrift, perhaps to drown in a sea of uncertainty, as the young woman in my office was discovering.

She and her husband had accomplished the first difficult steps toward discipline—they had made sincere commitments to each other and to their intimate relationship, and they had devised honest sets of priorities that each agreed upon.

Now they needed to understand the meaning of discipline, and to learn a few techniques to put it into effect.

Perhaps the most important and fundamental idea is simply that:

Discipline is control.

Throughout life, we unconsciously ask ourselves many questions. One of these is, "Do I take responsibility for myself and my relationship, or do I individually and cooperatively with my partner lose control?"

If you decline responsibility, you will have very bad discipline.

If you have very bad discipline, you will lose control. Very bad discipline is the discipline of aggression or withdrawal.

- Aggression happens when someone seeks to occupy by emotional or physical force somebody else's life space.

- Withdrawal happens when a partner simply bows out, becomes less than even an observer, blind to the relationship, as we saw in the preceding chapter.

Of course there are varying degrees of participation between these two unfortunate situations.

On the other hand, if you take responsibility and act on it, you have very good discipline.

If you have very good discipline, you gain increasing control.

Very good discipline happens when each person in a relationship remains in the appropriate life space while fulfilling the personal and relationship contracts. These contracts are based on the partners' individual expectations, commitments, and priorities, and they change and grow with the years.

Most people understand that discipline requires work. Unfortunately, a large number of people don't understand that the lack of discipline often requires much more work.

Without discipline, problems grow gigantic, distressful, out of control. Paralysis can spread to all areas of life. With discipline, problems are dealt with as they come up, leaving time, energy, and money to be used more appropriately—and happily—elsewhere.

If your driveway needs resurfacing and you have good discipline, you resurface the driveway.

To do that, you will have to make some choices. You may decide to deny yourself certain items in your budget so you can afford to do the resurfacing. Or if money is no problem, you will simply set aside time during your busy week to make the arrangements, take bids, decide on the materials, the contractor, and so forth. With discipline, you put in the necessary work, make the decisions, see the job to satisfying completion, and get on to more interesting aspects of life.

With bad discipline, the results are very different.

You may have good intentions, but little follow-through. You figure you'll get around to it eventually. Or you may avoid noticing the increasingly decrepit condition of the driveway. Eventually a big storm will wash away chunks. Your tires will get stuck in the holes, spin. More of the surface will erode. Asphalt will stick to your car, or concrete bits will knock the paint off. Neighborhood children and dogs may dig the holes deeper, wider. By the time you get around to doing something, you may have to tear up the old driveway and start from scratch. At this point, what was once a relatively simple job has become an outrageously expensive pain in the neck. Absurd? Yes, but believe me, these kinds of situations happen daily to people who are extremely conscientious and responsible in other areas of their lives.

In similar fashion, I am constantly impressed with the number of people who, when served with divorce papers, say with genuine hurt and bewilderment, "I had no idea there was anything wrong."

In terms of discipline, most people don't allow themselves to reach a stage of total disaster. Most eventually deal with problems, which means they have only partial losses of control.

But how much happier all of us would be if we would quickly recognize areas where changes needed to be made—stresses, remember?—and make the appropriate adjustments.

To shape our relationships into the kinds that are the most meaningful for us:

- We must be sufficiently disciplined to make a commitment even though we have no guarantee of the relationship's success.

- We must be sufficiently disciplined to reorganize our time so its use appropriately reflects our priorities.

- We must be sufficiently disciplined to reserve an appropriate amount of energy to nurture and enjoy our relationship.

- And we must be sufficiently disciplined to rearrange appropriately the ways in which we make, share, spend, save, and invest our money.

Discipline—like commitment—can mean freedom. Discipline makes taking control of your life possible.

There are three diverse techniques of intimacy discipline that I have found highly effective in creating the kind of healthy climate in which broken relationships can heal and sound relationships can grow and flourish. They are:

- The Sanctity of the Marriage Bed
- Conflict Resolution
- Forgiveness

As I describe each, please consider whether any of these areas cause problems in your life.

* * *

THE SANCTITY OF THE MARRIAGE BED

For ages the marriage bed has symbolized sanctuary, a safe haven from life's battlefields. Included in this important symbolism is also the quality of sanctity, that the marriage bed is inviolate.

For *marriage,* you may substitute *relationship,* and if you have no relationship *bed,* perhaps relationship *couch* is more appropriate.

But whatever words you choose, you can designate a place in your home as a sanctuary for your marriage or relationship, a safe harbor, and you can insist the sanctuary be inviolate.

No matter what happens in the world outside, no matter what happens in the other rooms of your house, you can choose to allow nothing negative to violate your haven. If you do this, only positive experiences—at the worst, neutral experiences—will happen there.

> We will not fight in our bedroom; that doesn't mean we mustn't fight, only that we won't fight here. Instead here we will sleep, which is a refreshment. Here we will dream, inviting our unconsciouses to come alive. Here we will make love, joining in the wonderful sacrament God gave us. Here we will be close, com-

muning and communicating in love. Our bedroom is a place for
our refreshment, integration, and closeness. It is our sanctuary.

Safety and security are vital to all humans, and the most vital kinds
of safety and security are those we carry within us. With a sanctuary built of intimate love, brought to physical recognition by the
walls of your shared room, you have a guaranteed location in
which to fulfill this very human need. Here you can leave the world
and its problems behind. Here you can safely grow your love.

One remarkable technique to help this along is what I call the
poem of the marriage bed. Perhaps you'd like to try it.

Every night as you hold each other before sleep, think of what
your partner has said or done to show you in the course of the day
that he or she loves you. It's a simple thing to do.

> "I felt loved by you today. You put a flower in my appointment
> book, and every time I opened the book, I saw it and felt won-
> derful."

> "I felt loved by you today. I know how busy you are, but you
> called me just to see how I was getting along."

> "I felt loved by you today. I loved the very expensive bottle of
> perfume you bought me, but I also loved the note you wrote me,
> which was a very expensive thought."

Like all poetry, the poem of the marriage bed is an art based on
craft and refined lovingly into illumination and beauty.

Anyone can learn the craft of being thoughtful and caring.
People in the health care fields do it all the time.

Only intimate love can raise the craft above the mundane.
With intimate love, caring is full of revelation and meaning, and
the partners involved are transformed.

In the poem of the marriage bed, very amazing changes begin
to occur.

> You begin to look for ways in which your partner is saying "I
> love you" nonverbally.

You begin to look for ways to show your love for your partner.

Your feelings of being loved grow and grow.

Your desire to love in return grows and grows.

This is not a transactional relationship. It doesn't mean that if I tell you three things tonight and you tell me only one, then you owe me two extras tomorrow night.

No, this is definitely not a transactional relationship.

Instead this is a straight, no-strings-attached gift each of you gives yourself and the other.

Let's say that every night you and your partner reflect upon two or three examples of loving each experienced from the other during the day. In the course of a week, each of you would have eighteen or so instances of being loved. In the course of a month, you would have sixty or ninety. And in a year, a thousand ways in which your partner has shown you love.

Although the numbers are impressive, the cumulative effect is perhaps even more significant. Here you are building a bank account against the crises and negativity that each of us experiences simply by living. With this technique, the third person in your relationship grows stronger, and consequently you and your partner do, too.

This can be a very dramatic way to resuscitate dying relationships.

This also creates a rich environment in which to continue to grow your relationship in the ways most meaningful to you and your partner.

CHAPTER 14

DISCIPLINE— CONFLICT RESOLUTION & FORGIVENESS

> Psychological insecurity, however, increases in proportion to social security, unconsciously at first, causing neuroses, then consciously, bringing with it separations, discord, divorces, and other marital disorders.
>
> —C.G. JUNG
> *Marriage as a Psychological Relationship*

The man's face was red, furious with anger. He sat in my office, gripping the arms of his chair until his knuckles turned white. "She's done it again," he said, his words clipped, harsh. "I won't take it anymore. Drinking! The kids are a mess. I haven't been able to talk to her—really talk to her—in years. We don't have any friends left. This is it. I'm leaving!"

His words, his face, his whole demeanor cried out in anguish. We try. God knows how hard we try to make our relationships work.

Just as most relationship problems have no simple solutions, most also have very complicated causes. This was true of my new client's situation. Years of accumulated inability to show love, communicate, resolve problems, wipe away pain, and forgive one another had at last erupted in the death throes of his long-term marriage.

He and his wife had tried to the best of their abilities with the tools at their disposal, and still the marriage had failed. As he, and eventually his ex-wife, learned in their individual therapies, ignorance is not always bliss. With information we can short-circuit problems; we can deal with them.

Problem solving takes many qualities, and chief among them is discipline. We've talked about one technique of discipline—what I call the sanctity of the marriage bed—and now we're going to explore two more:

- Conflict Resolution
- Forgiveness

CONFLICT RESOLUTION

To survive, a marriage or significant relationship must have methods for processing disagreement. One of the first tests we can apply to the health of a relationship is not so much whether there are conflicts, but whether those conflicts are addressed and resolved. Is a conclusion brought to the conflict, or are the ends left dangling, waiting to fuel the next inevitable disagreement?

There's an old saying that goes something like this: "How do I know what I think if I don't have someone with whom I can argue about it?"

The presence of conflict, particularly in the early stages of a relationship, is necessary. It is like the need of a plant for a bigger pot. Too many people throw out their plants when all that is needed is transplanting to larger pots. When plants grow, they need more space, more air, more water, more nutrients.

And so with a marriage or committed relationship, many people tend to throw out the living plant when all that's wrong is that the environment has become too small.

What happens when a relationship is living in a space so small that expansion and growth are impossible? A similar situation occurs when a macaw lives in a parakeet's cage. The macaw won't have enough space. It will turn upon itself, jab and peck and destroy, quite literally eat itself away.

Conflict in some marriages becomes very much like this, gnawing away at the heart of the relationship until it destroys itself and the relationship.

But this doesn't have to happen. Instead conflict can serve the useful purposes it was intended to have. It can provide opportunities to understand one another, clarify thinking, resolve differences, and move closer to the unified, committed relationships that are the best for us.

There are two major areas of conflict resolution:

- Fact
- Opinion

Did it rain a week ago last Saturday? A simple question, but such simple questions are surprisingly difficult for many couples to answer. This is because the form has taken over the substance. Their conflicts contain ready-made anger, fueled by the frustration of having unresolved conflicts from the past.

The first approach to resolving conflicts is to ask yourself whether there is a factual, ascertainable answer to the question that is being argued about.

If there is, then blow the whistle. Go to the encyclopedia or the newspaper or the library or call a friend. Find out the answer to the question. Then relax and smile. You have both won. You've resolved your conflict.

The issue isn't to prove who is right or who is wrong.

The issue isn't to punish the other person.

Instead the issue is simply to answer the question.

* * *

The second area of conflict resolution is not as easily dealt with. This area is one of opinion. Here your opinion is just as good as mine, and mine is just as good as yours. The fact that we disagree on an issue of principle need not break up our relationship. Instead our ability to disagree will affirm our togetherness as well as our individuality.

Whether the issue is politics, religion, sex, or money, I hope each of you feels comfortable expressing your views with the intimate person in your life.

As long as there is love, you can communicate anything.

When there isn't love, you can communicate very little.

Every relationship needs a method to deal with conflicts of opinion and principle. The best way to begin is by inviting the other person's views, listening with respect and attention. When your partner is finished, then you have your turn, stating your opinion as clearly and persuasively as possible. Neither of you ever stoops to personal attacks, not only because insults and bullying are ineffective arguments, but also because you have too much love and respect for one another to cause such painful damage.

After that, you take turns arguing the issue back and forth. More ideas will occur to both of you. Your thinking will muddy and clarify. Perhaps one of you will persuade the other, and in that case you can both feel triumphant because your work has brought resolution.

But more likely, you will not change your partner's mind, and your partner will not change yours. And that is fine, too, a resolution in itself if you recognize the love and respect you share. You are not clones of one another. You are not in competition. Instead you are living with an exciting person who is an individual thinker, someone to be admired.

* * *

There remains one more area of conflict resolution that falls in the classification of opinion, but it is a much more potentially dangerous area than those we've been discussing. It often deals with ethical or moral issues.

This kind of conflict cannot be resolved factually, and it may not be resolvable in terms of live and let live—*I respect your opinion, and you respect my opinion, and so we will go on our ways rejoicing while still seeking to convert the other person to common sense and reason.*

No, I'm referring to issues of such moral significance they absolutely curdle your blood or the blood of the other person. They are issues one or both cannot live with, issues such as whether sexual relationships outside the marriage are all right.

In my experience, such painful conflicts arise relatively rarely. When they do occur, however, discussion often brings no resolution, compromise, or acceptance of the other person's position. Then the conflict-resolution process has disintegrated into impossibility.

At this unhappy point many people hide from reality. There is silence, no communication about the issue at all. And that causes cancer in a relationship.

A cancer in a relationship occurs when an issue exists—and it can be a simple issue, by the way—that cannot be communicated. Untreated, the cancer will spread to other issues, grow so large it can kill the relationship. This is the dominant reason relationships fail from conflict of opinion.

A relationship filled with recurrent pain needs help. No matter how willing and dedicated the partners are, their capability to communicate and resolve ongoing issues has been exceeded. A professional therapist might help them to decide whether a pulse of life still beats in their relationship, and then to get on with rebuilding their lives—either together or separately.

But before the pain reaches the recurrent stage, the wisest solution to the breakdown is resumed communication, no matter how difficult the subject matter.

Communication and conflict resolution are acts of discipline, and with them you can regain control of your life.

As long as there is love with your communication, you can talk more and more. Peeling away the layers of fear and distress can reveal the heart of the difficult issue. Remember each of us has our own sets of fears and uncertainties, our own inner messages and expectations. As you talk about those, you'll rediscover each other, find new ways to view your ongoing conflict. Ideas will occur to you. Possible solutions. As you move closer together, you also will move closer to the answers that are right for you.

With love, anything is possible, even the resolution of seemingly hopeless conflicts.

FORGIVENESS

In the techniques of discipline, perhaps the most important, most difficult, and most elusive of all is forgiveness. And yet, its rewards may be the greatest.

Forgiveness doesn't mean avoidance. It doesn't mean denial. It doesn't mean wiping the event or events from your memory. How can you forget what has been?

Forgiveness encompasses infidelity and instances of humiliation, discourtesy and disrespect, minor slights and wicked talk, and even what is perhaps the greatest of all sins in a relationship—indifference.

Now I'd like you to do something for yourself. Think of some of the things in your primary relationship that you honestly feel you cannot forgive.

If you don't want to write a list, then please make a mental one. Take all the time you need. This is for your information alone. As we continue with the section, your list may be helpful to you.

* * *

Few people deliberately set out to cause others pain, and yet it happens. Some people are genuinely sorry afterwards. Others don't know they've caused a hurt. And still others recognize the damage they've done, but for one reason or another don't care.

Generally we find forgiving a person easiest when they sincerely regret the transgression and when we believe the offense will not happen again.

After that we begin to have problems.

- How do you forgive the one-night affair your partner has with your best friend?

- How do you forgive the ongoing lack of respect in your marriage that your partner tries to cover with monetary gifts?

- How do you forgive your partner's alcoholism and the daily abuse that goes with it?

- How do you forgive lies?

- How do you forgive incest?

These are enormous questions. Before answering "how," let's begin with "why."

Why should anyone forgive?

The simplest, most trivial sin can be unforgiveable. *If you step on my toe, it is unforgiveable unless I choose to forgive you. But I have to forgive you, and so I will. If you steal something from me, which is much more serious, I have to forgive you. I really have to because I cannot afford not to. I cannot carry the weight of bitterness. My wallet may be lighter, but what I would take away from your theft would be much heavier, and that would be my refusal to forgive you.*

An unforgiven transgression is a magnet for anger and bitterness.

The anger and bitterness will definitely settle on you, not necessarily on the person who has hurt you.

Your unresolved emotions will become your iron prison, encasing you in preconceived attitudes that will color the rest of your life.

If the transgressions you cannot forgive constitute even 1 percent of your intimate relationship, they will eventually taint the other 99 percent, in the end dooming your entire relationship to an angry and bitter death.

Another reason to forgive is that hurting someone else will not heal your wounds.

Only forgiveness will heal your wounds.

This is true even in the most grievous, the most abusive situations.

Understanding why abusive situations happen is helpful. Abuse is almost always a symptom of the abuser's emotional deprivation. The deprivation may have begun in childhood, during adolescence, or even during an early love relationship or marriage. Most likely the deprivation fed upon itself, causing the pain to accumulate. When this happens, people feel as if they have enormous aching holes in them, holes they believe they have the right —and they do indeed have the right—to have filled. So they set out to fill them. Some people try food, drugs, alcohol, or sex. Others become physically or emotionally cruel to others. But none of this works. None of us can make ourselves happy by hurting ourselves or by hurting others.

Forgiving a person who continues to abuse you is a lot to ask. But to heal yourself, you must. You do not, however, have to put up with the abuse.

If the need to inflict pain in a relationship is recurrent and life-threatening, the relationship is over. The message is clearly that if the relationship isn't going to die, then you will. In this extreme form of recurrently produced pain, I'd get out of the relationship. I'd remove myself as a target.

In less threatening situations such as alcoholism and drug abuse, I'd put a deadline on the behavior, and I'd make it a relatively short deadline, especially if physical violence or the potential of physical violence exists. The next time the abuse happens should be the last time because that's the time to walk away.

But still, to save myself, I'd forgive my partner.

None of us needs the anger, bitterness, self-righteousness, and feelings of powerlessness that are the human residue of these horrible situations.

To forgive does not mean to forget.

Forgiveness means remembering and letting go. Forgiveness means cleansing yourself of pain, anger, and humiliation. Forgiveness means purifying yourself so you can get on with life.

There is life after forgiveness, and it is a wonderfully good life, perhaps better than any you've ever known. And this can be true in every situation, whether you and your partner have broken up, or whether you and your partner have resolved your differences and are continuing on a more appropriate and happy relationship path.

* * *

How does one forgive?

First by confronting the reality. Why are you so dreadfully

hurt by what has been done to you by this person who claims to love you? When you confront the issue both on a superficial and then on an in-depth level, you can begin to make attitudinal changes.

For recurrent hurts, the attitudes of both people must change. Once attitudes have changed, then behavior can be changed so that the offenses will stop.

And so those of us who want to forgive or be forgiven can begin by facing one another. How wonderful it is for a couple to sit together with honesty.

> "This thing is causing trouble between us. You may not know it. You may not even remember it. But it is before me night and day. When you do certain things, you push my replay button, and a tape comes on and says, 'Remember that? That's happened before!' I remember that look as if it were yesterday. I remember that tone of voice, those words. I remember the lies you told me. I remember all those things, and they are a sword through my heart as fresh as if it were happening right now!"

> "I'm sorry. I hope you can forgive me. I don't want to hurt you anymore. I will try never again to let those things happen. I hope that if I somehow slip and you should see me fall into old ways, that you will help me to stand on my feet again. I love you. I don't want to lose you. Our relationship is so important to me that I will work very hard to change."

Openness is the key, the heart of forgiveness. By talking honestly and with love, we pull out the sting from the memory so that the awfulness can fade into obscurity, never again to be enlivened by leftover pain and bitterness.

The result is forgiveness.

Forgiveness means putting something away.

It means drawing a line under something and saying, "Finished."

Whatever the horror, whatever the nightmare, it's over because it's forgiven.

The courage to forgive is gigantic, and the courage to acknowledge the need to forgive or to be forgiven is perhaps even greater.

* * *

It takes a big person to forgive, but it sometimes takes an even bigger person to accept forgiveness. At the heart of experiencing forgiveness is the willingness to acknowledge wrongdoing and the desire to be forgiven.

In our society, atonement is built into wrong-doing. If we do something wrong—hurt someone—we and others often expect us to make atonement.

The difficult part for a person who is forgiven is to realize that forgiveness is not a transaction. If the person whom I wronged forgives me, I really do not have to prove that I am worthy of forgiveness.

No one can earn forgiveness.

There is nothing anyone can do to buy forgiveness.

Receiving this kind of free, unencumbered gift in a you-get-what-you-pay-for society is difficult to believe.

But for the person who has committed the wrong-doing, accepting forgiveness and then, ultimately, self-forgiveness leads to freedom from past mistakes.

Just as true forgiveness wipes the slate clean for the person who forgives, true forgiveness also wipes the slate clean for the wrongdoer. This person has a fresh beginning, an opportunity to get on with life in a wiser, healthier, more meaningful way.

* * *

How does a person learn to forgive?

You learn to forgive just as you learn to love. You simply go ahead and do it.

You feel awkward, uncertain, even bumbling, but still your mouth forms the words, your heart opens, and you forgive the person who has hurt you. It is a remarkably cleansing feeling.

This is the same way you accept forgiveness. You don't have

to analyze it, or particularly understand it, but you do need to try out the feelings of forgiveness. Let them slowly grow on you. Allow yourself to shed your guilt, your need to make atonement. Move on with life, recognizing the goodness in yourself, and you harm yourself when you harm others. Forgiveness helps you to be free to not do that anymore.

The ideal situation is when you and your partner can sit down together and discuss the hurts that one of you has inflicted on the other. As you reveal yourselves, the one who needs to can sincerely ask forgiveness while the other just as sincerely can give it.

Unfortunately, this ideal situation is not always possible.

Sometimes the person whose harm was the most grievous to us is unreachable, perhaps even dead. Or sometimes the person won't talk to us, doesn't feel the need to be forgiven at all. And sometimes the person blames us for whatever happened and will have nothing to do with us.

In any case, we realize we still carry the hurt, that we now may have some bitterness and anger because of it. This is negative, excess emotional baggage, and it is bound to affect our present intimate relationship, probably more than we realize.

We know whatever the other person thinks or feels, the time has come for us to forgive.

And we can do that. We can write the person a letter, pouring out our feelings and remembrances. We don't have to mail the letter, just write it. Likewise we can tell our partner or another sympathetic listener about the incident or incidents, filling in the details as completely as possible.

After we have said everything we can think to say, after we have wept and raged because in painful situations people often need to weep and rage, we can know we have begun the difficult but growthful process of forgiving.

* * *

The lack of forgiveness is one of the biggest obstacles to happiness in a relationship. When nonforgiveness begins, relationship growth stops, and often personal growth as well.

Please look at the list you made of incidents and events you haven't forgiven. If you did not make a list, you may wish to do so now. Think carefully about each unforgiven item.

Arrange them from easiest to most difficult to forgive.

Now look at the easiest and think carefully about it. Feel your emotions.

Next look at the most difficult and think carefully about it. Feel your emotions again.

Notice how your emotions are the same for the easiest incident as for the most difficult, only the intensity differs.

When you are ready to heal yourself, you can go to work.

I suggest you begin with the easiest item you have listed. Forgiving the person who has wronged you will take tremendous courage. Use whatever methods seem most appropriate to you—letter writing, talking, prayer, inner monologue, or even showering—but do please cleanse yourself.

Forgiveness will put an end to your suffering over this event or events.

Forgiveness is an act of discipline, of your regaining control over your life.

Once you begin, you can work your way through the rest of the list, forgiving at your own pace.

The courageous act of forgiveness causes a wide door to swing open to the world, and through this door you can find peace.

I'm sure that all of us have forgiven, sometimes at great cost, and I'm equally sure that unfortunately all of us sometimes have not forgiven. When you compare the payoff between what happens when you forgive and what happens when you don't forgive, the act of forgiveness becomes imperative.

When we find peace, it settles in our hearts and spreads to the rest of our lives. It nurtures us, our partner, our relationship, and those around us. Peace is love's natural environment, and in this environment intimate relationships heal and flourish.

CHAPTER 15

INTIMACIES—
EVER-WIDENING DIMENSIONS
OF LOVE

Looking outwards has got to be turned into looking into oneself. Discovering yourself provides you with all you are, were meant to be, and all you are living from and for.

—C.G. JUNG
C.G. Jung Speaking

Recently I worked with a very special woman who was terminally ill. Throughout her three-month hospitalization many people heard about her and came to know her. Doctors, nurses, health technicians, and janitors would stop to chat with her because she was so incredible. Many brought other patients to meet her. I'll call her Joan.

Joan would tell all of them, "I thank God for this disease because it has transformed my life."

When people first heard her, they were shocked. We are not prepared to have the dying tell us they are glad to have the illness that is killing them. Yet for her own personal reasons this remarkable woman, who courageously chose to transform her fear of death into a celebration of life, was saying exactly that—and much more.

Joan's hospital room was always filled with flowers. Her husband, Jack, had arranged family photographs on a cabinet and her favorite pictures on the white walls. Her bed was beside the window. She lay in the bed, propped up, and the sunlight streamed through the window, igniting her blue eyes as she talked. When she was without pain, she was radiant.

This is her story:

My priorities in life have changed. It took this disease to show me what really matters.

The only thing that the money we've accumulated has done is to give me a private room. That's all. I'm not getting any better medical attention than anyone else—there isn't any better available, and fortunately everyone has access to it.

Now that time is short for me, I'm doing the things I put off for years. There is so much I want to do.

The books I've always intended to read I'm reading now. The poetry I've always wanted to write I'm writing now. The forgiveness I needed to give to others and to receive myself I really am giving—and receiving. And I can at last tell my family and friends, whom I love so much, that I love them.

The sort of person that I always wanted to be I'm becoming.

Although I'm not happy to be dying, I'm proud of myself, and very glad to be me. You may think this is strange, you probably don't understand a word I'm saying, but all of this is true.

Of all my changes, the most important—the one that has brought me happiness I never thought possible—has been in my relationship with Jack.

Jack has never been so loving. Yet for years he neglected me. Then this happened. Jack could have deserted me. Instead he's stayed with me through everything.

He spends time with me, which somehow he's managed to take away from his work. We're together three or four hours every day in the hospital. We hold hands and talk. We laugh a lot. We enjoy each other.

We reminisce about everything that's happened over the years. I'm seeing our experiences from his perspective. Now I understand more about him and us. We also talk about the meaning of life and death, and how love seems to transcend it all.

Every night he brushes my hair. He has very gentle hands now. He hasn't brushed my hair for fifteen years. It took this disease, and he's brushed my hair every night for the last two months. He's told me that he loves me more often in the last two months than he's told me in the last fifteen years. And I tell him often that I love him. But how I wish the words were really enough to describe my limitless feelings for him!

Because I'm fortunate to have this private room, Jack can sleep with me. We lie together and breathe as if we were one person, one shared spirit. I marvel that I'd thought our relationship was dead. Now I see life was there all along.

I think if I hadn't had this disease he and I would have just continued on like wooden puppets. We would have always been half dead in the midst of physical health. Now our marriage is fully alive in the presence of my illness. Isn't it sad to think of the people who are still living the way we used to?

Remembering what we were before makes me grateful for the time I have left—I have Jack, and at last I know how to live.

* * *

I wish I could say Joan survived. It is a loss for all of us that she did not. One evening she passed quietly from this life into the next, and Jack was with her, holding her hand.

I will never forget Joan, nor will the people whom she touched with the openness and wisdom that grew from her tragedy. Joan left a great legacy—a cherished life. We should not forget what she and others have struggled so hard to learn. Remembering can help us to transform our own relationships—and lives.

* * *

Intimacy is the most pleasurable state of being that humans are capable of experiencing.

Alcohol, cocaine, winning elections, accruing money and corporate power—all are far outdistanced by the deep, continuous emotional joy that comes from intimate relationships.

That's why we humans in our stubborn, clumsy, pitiful, and adorable ways keep searching for intimacy. Even the most hopeless among us—those of us who say "It's over, I'll never find anyone, and I don't want to find anyone!"—still are aware of love relationships around us, still look at people we find attractive and speculate about the possibilities with this person or that person. Even when we feel locked forever into a dead relationship, our minds wander and wonder.

The human spirit is indomitable, which Joan exemplified so well.

But intimacy as a concept can be overwhelming in its magnitude. It can arouse tremendous fears, such as of rejection, abandonment, failure, and success. It can seem too big and tall a mountain to scale. It can seem too elusive a quest to be worth the effort. Intimacy can be so awesome that we shun its pursuit, or we set ourselves up to fail at it.

To counteract our fears, Joan reminded us of a very important, fundamental lesson—that intimacies (plural) partake of, and together create, the way of life we call intimacy.

Intimacies are intimacy in miniature.

Intimacies individually are what the whole of intimacy looks like, feels like, and sounds like.

Intimacies are the seemingly small acts of everyday life that say in words and deeds that I love you.

They are brushing your beloved's hair, wiping her face, fetching the nurse. They are hanging pictures on the wall and arranging photographs on cabinets and shelves. They are sharing your laughter, dreams, fears, and memories. And they are saying the words: "I love you."

At the beginning of a relationship, intimacies are easy. They speak in poetry, in flowers, in politeness, in exquisite courtesy, in all of the myriad small and grand gestures of relating.

But after a while, what happens to the courtesies, the attentiveness, the gifts of love and time? What happens to the desire to show the central person in your life that he or she is special?

Relationships are not just for use on Sunday outings. They cannot survive if they are preserved only to gather dust behind the glass of courtship's distant past.

Relationships—like people—must live in the real world of today's needs and emotions. Sometimes in a relationship, oneself is the loneliest person in the world. Sometimes we can give intimacies to others, but for one reason or another can accept none in return.

So if you happen to be alone or to feel alone, what I'm describing applies to you, too.

When were you last graciously intimate with yourself?

In the following pages you'll find a drug-free prescription that can work miracles in replacing relationship distress with happiness.

It is a prescription of words with very practical meanings, and they will be familiar to you because we've already discussed many in this book. I invite you to apply generously the meaning of each to yourself and to the central person in your life.

As part of the prescription, please consider the role each of the following intimacy experiences already plays in your life.

Ask yourself: When did I last have the experience? When did I last generate it? Would I like it? With whom could I have it? And then, because no one can do it for you, and because every single one of us deserves the absolutely best of life, please go for it!

* * *

Intimacies mean **touching** and being touched. Those are simple intimacies. You don't touch everybody, and everybody doesn't touch you. But with the right person, there are so many different ways for me to touch you and for you to touch me intimately. You touch my heart—that's an intimacy. You touch my mind. You touch my soul. You touch me.

I was deeply touched by what you said. I was immensely moved by what you did. Thank you for touching me so deeply, not with your hands necessarily—although that's nice, too—but with yourself. You touch me with an angel's kiss, and you reach my very soul.

Tenderness. Tenderness is very intimate. You can't have intimacy without tenderness. The gentility of tender affection, the graciousness of tender words, the loveliness of a tender attitude— that's intimacy. When was somebody really tender to you last? When were you tender to someone else? When did you last speak tenderly to somebody? When did you last take the time to be tender?

Laughing and **crying.** Many relationships that I see professionally don't laugh very much anymore. There's some crying, to be sure. In a relationship where there's little laughter, almost certainly there's going to be some crying because crying tends to fill the vacuum laughter leaves.

There's intimate crying, and there's separation crying. Not all crying is intimate, and not all laughter is intimate. Often the differences are difficult to perceive. Under the guise of laughing with you, I might laugh at you, and that's not tender, not gracious, and certainly not intimate. Instead, that's destructive and hostile. That pulls you—and, ultimately, us—down.

But intimacy always lifts us up. Laughing with you is intimate. In a crowded room where we're ever so formal, our gazes touch and there's a little dance of laughter in our eyes—that's very intimate. Or a tear glistens that no one else notices, but I share it with you because we know one another so deeply, so well—that's wonderfully intimate.

Do you see that every single word that I'm prescribing is capable of abuse? In some relationships a subtle alchemy in reverse begins to happen. The form of the intimacies continues long after the substance has died. And so we laugh together, but I'm laughing at you now. And we cry together, but we're crying because of each other. And I touch you, but no longer very gently, tenderly, or intimately. I touch to ward you off, because if I don't I'll crash into you in the corridor.

Talking can be an intensely intimate form of **communication**, but it also can be brutal. You cannot have intimacy without communication, and in my experience the number one problem in the breakdown of most relationships is the breakdown of communication. This doesn't happen necessarily because the two people don't talk anymore, but because of what they talk about, don't talk about, and the way in which they talk, if they talk at all.

And so, as you can see, **silence** can be a symptom of the comfortableness of our intimacy, or it can be a symptom of our withdrawal from pain.

Giving and **receiving** are as important as the give and take of life itself. Gifts that buy people are not intimate. Gifts that cost nothing of the inner self are not intimate. But a gift that comes from the mind, the heart, the soul shows the value the giver places on the relationship. Being able to receive a gift with the full acceptance of the love and caring that went into it infuses the relationship with joy, a reflection of the gift itself.

In intimacy, you and I will have **confidence** in one another. We take the **risk** of **being vulnerable**, of **being open**, because we have no fear the other will use our **secrets** to their advantage. I **trust** you, which doesn't mean you're never going to hurt me. You probably will, and, in our openness, I will probably hurt you. But my **intentions** are never to do so, and I trust that your intentions are never to hurt me either. And so, in that sense, even our hurts become intimacies.

We know **pain** and **pleasure**, so intimate, also can be used cruelly. Pain inflicted on another is not intimate. Pain shared with another can be profoundly intimate. When I share my inner pleasures with you and you ignore or ruin them, you are denying my honest experience. Pleasure gained at the partner's expense or disregarding the partner's feelings is not intimate. But when each of us revels in the other's happinesses, our relationship grows strong in happiness, too.

Likewise, the greater the content of intimacy in our **sexuality**, the greater the joy that will fill our relationship.

Sex as a weapon is violence. But sex as a shared, exciting, deeply loving experience is a sacrament.

Respect is an attitude for which **courtesy** is an expression. My courteous behavior to you is a sign of my respect for you. My respect is an acceptance of your **autonomy,** of the uniqueness of you. I am **honest** with you because I respect you, and in return you can feel safe being honest with me. Who would want to live with someone whom they didn't respect?

Is intimacy possible? Despite all the shoddiness in the world around us, people ask, is love between two humans really possible? Yes, but you have to have faith that it is. Faith is an intimacy—faith in oneself, in each other, in the ability to love and be loved. Love cannot be proved, but the truth of love emerges as an ongoing response to intimacies if you have the faith to keep with it.

And love does mean having to say you're sorry—often! **Apologies** given and received are difficult to come by in some relationships, and those relationships will increasingly ail. No relationship can exist without **forgiveness** because no relationship can exist without hurt. As Henri J.M. Nouwen has written in his book *Intimacy,* "Love is an act of forgiving in which evil is converted into good, and destruction into creation."

You can't have intimacy without **surrender.** There are many ways of surrendering, but for each to be an act of intimacy all must take place in **safety,** not in capitulation. Surrender is safe if it's done not in the fear of darkness, but in the light of a welcoming love.

A good **argument** can be extremely intimate. Sharing the intimacy of **ideas,** allowing your ideas to rub against the ideas of your partner—this is a very human and important endeavor. And, of course, it is always done to resolve issues, not to punish.

Can you imagine a relationship succeeding in which **promises** were not kept? Love, trust, belief, respect, joy—all are founded on promises. Inherent in any intimate relationship are certain promises—spoken and unspoken—and those promises are basically to adhere to the **expectations** each partner brings into a relationship. One of those unspoken expectations might be **fidelity, faithfulness.**

Breaking promises can lead to the breakdown of the relationship.

Of the people I see, I find generally that a woman's expectations for her primary relationship are much more profound than are a man's. I believe this one-sidedness situation arises from cultural attitudes, and we have discussed this at greater length earlier in the book. Still, I want to reiterate here the importance of both people sharing early in the relationship what their expectations are, and then to continue to share them throughout their years together.

Sharing and negotiating expectations is a vital intimacy.

Otherwise, what tends to happen is that the woman ends up with the short end of the relationship stick. As the man becomes more and more enveloped in business, in the nature of things the woman—not all, but a very large number of women—becomes more enveloped in the family, despite her outside work. And he has his life, and she has hers. Often by the third or fourth year they no longer have the time, the communication skills, the **discipline**, the **priority**, and the **commitment** to bridge the gap.

At this point the relationship is in real trouble. Most people who bring this problem to me are women, primarily because men tend to find alternative compensations in their larger worlds. He works harder, gets more money, more prestige, more promotions, more opportunities to meet with and expand his interest group, which buys him time to ignore his problems at home. Meanwhile, she frequently has access only to the circumscribed world in which she finds herself imprisoned.

She feels guilty about her unhappiness, isolation, and loneliness. Isn't she supposed to be here? Isn't he supposed to be there? Many women have said to me, "He works so hard he has no time for me." One woman told me, "I'd rather deal with a mistress than with that wonderful profession of his. It robs me of him, robs the kids of him, robs our life of intimacy. After five years of marriage I'm living in a shell."

Today many divorced men wander the streets and sidewalks of their lives in bewilderment. "What happened?" they ask. "I did everything I was supposed to do, but she divorced me. Now I have a new car, a new girlfriend. Why aren't I happy?"

Intimacies, remember? The little acts of everyday life that show the central person in your existence that they are not only important, but irreplaceable.

You can buy a new car, find a new lover, even marry a new spouse, but until intimacies become integral to your life, you won't have the transformational joy and fulfillment of intimacy itself. Until you give your relationship the same respect you give your work, you won't make a success of intimacy.

And if you don't respect your work, don't respect your intimate partner, what or whom do you respect?

Your **attitude** does count.

Love, like grace and forgiveness, is a gift. You can never earn the **gift of love**. There is no cost; love is a pearl beyond price.

Trying to prove you are worth being loved is a very forlorn endeavor.

Tragically, many people make a career of doing so. They often use sex as a compensation, which after a while becomes routine, boring for them—one seed of the apple cannot take the place of the whole apple. If life is indeed a transaction, which many people believe, then you get what you're worth, and if you're worth nothing then certainly you'll get nothing, especially not love and intimacy.

All of the intimacies about which we've been talking work toward one particular end—specialness.

"You are really special to me." Have you heard that lately? However casual or intense a relationship, whether it is between a man and a woman, a husband and a wife, lovers, men and men, women and women, or parent and child—intimacies say and show in a multitude of ways you are special to me.

How can I love when I don't know anybody to love? The answer is simple, yet difficult if you're out of practice: You begin by loving yourself.

Intimacies, which are the fruits of intimacy, can enliven loneliness. We can have numerous intimate experiences with ourselves —physically, spiritually, and emotionally. A walk in the park, a greeting card that we send ourselves, a bouquet of flowers, a loving smile in the mirror, the warm glow that comes from the self-appreciation of a job well done—these are dimensions of loving that are surely among the most neglected.

Too frequently the very last recipient on our intimacy gift wish list is ourselves. But every word in our prescription—tenderness, courtesy, respect, touching, giving, receiving, laughter, and all the rest—are gifts of loving we can bestow upon ourselves.

And unless we do so, giving those intimacies to others is going to be extremely difficult, except as empty compensatory gestures.

In an intimate relationship, the key to unhappiness is often ourselves. Women as well as men are bewildered by their lack of intimacy. Accepting responsibility is important. Blaming others for our deprivations won't fill the void.

Sometimes we're afflicted with what I call metaphorically an emotional equivalent of AIDS—an Acquired Immune Deficiency Syndrome that depletes and ultimately destroys our emotional lives. It's acquired by long deprivation, by being the recipient of acts of cruelty, of neglect, of being ignored, of being treated like a piece of furniture, a nonperson. It comes from being treated with contempt, with disdain, of being put down, of being the object of indifference.

Violence in a relationship doesn't always involve the fist.

Cruelty, like intimacy, can be extremely subtle.

When this particular kind of metaphorical AIDS settles into your emotional immune system, you grow increasingly incapable of resisting the large and small onslaughts of reality.

Eventually, like the common cold is to a person who is afflicted by the terrible physical disease called AIDS, a little insult becomes a crushing emotional blow. The emotional cold and the emotional influenza weaken you until you go down more and more often for less and less reason.

The good news is that *emotional* acquired immune deficiency is curable. I have seen people who were almost terminally ill emotionally—who were so low they wanted to die—who brought themselves up from the hopeless depths through the power of intimacy, through the same ordinary acts that we've been talking about here—courtesy, trust, talking, respect, and so forth.

I've seen relationships and marriages suffering from emotional acquired immune deficiency recover miraculously with the liberal application of intimacies.

The healing power of love is beyond our comprehension.

When you're in love, nothing can withstand its power. Slowly with the application of intimacies the two people grow stronger and stronger until they are able to withstand the normal slings and arrows of everyday misfortune.

There's no such thing as a little intimacy or an insignificant intimacy. There's only the big picture; a seemingly little intimacy contains all the elements of the entire concept, the entire way of life, the power of intimacy.

Intimacy is the freeway along which love drives, and love casts out fear, worthlessness, and hopelessness.

Slowly, ever so slowly, the intimacies mount up. The gift of intimacy is irresistible; it eventually wears down even the hardest heart. With intimacies, the frightened child within can mature through experience. And this is the healing power of love.

* * *

Intimacy is a miracle. Yet it is a miracle as birth and healing are miracles. We don't know why a broken bone heals, and we don't know how to make it happen. It's a miracle of nature, something unexplainable that works for our good. And so intimacy in that sense is a miracle.

Intimacy requires flying in the face of so much of what we think of as human nature. It means flying in the face of selfishness, greed, ego, and power—all false gods to which we in our ignorance and weakness often unknowingly dedicate our lives.

Intimacy means forgiving the unforgivable, supporting the unsupportable. It means seeing the world almost upside down. Love transforms and clarifies the universe that we thought we saw. Intimacy means moving out of the range of the unconscious and its shadows, and into the clear light of consciousness with all its choices, freedom, and fulfillment.

No other animal can approach the levels of love and voluntary self-sacrifice that a human can. And no other animal is as culpably evil as is the human being. We're both of these things at once.

And as we grow older, we begin to realize we have a choice between our tendency toward culpable evil and our miraculous capacity for healing love.

We find that, as we move—sometimes extremely painfully and uncertainly—along our conscious paths seeking intimacy, the rewards are so immense that turning back into the darkness of our unconsciouses becomes unthinkable.

This is a great mystery, the transformation that comes from intimate love. Yet it is an experience that each of us can have, indeed needs to have, as the individual and collective scripts that we write for ourselves change our lives—and the world.

INTIMACY WORKBOOK

YOUR AGENDA FOR CHANGE

Without being aware of it, we humans are controlled by the unconscious even while we are exercising our greatest freedoms of choice.

We are the supreme paradox.

We are controlled by unconscious forces that pull us down and inundate us. Yet we are capable of transcendence in the experience of loving another.

Consider some of the couples we met in this book—Charlie and Kate who battled his testing disease, the Tinleys whose marriage at last exploded in violence, the newlyweds Eric and Pauline whose vision of a lifelong honeymoon ended abruptly in frustration and furious silence.

In each relationship, the partners' unconscious fears and motivations were destroying—or had destroyed—fulfilling intimacy.

As we've discussed in this book, we human beings have a built-in eraser on the blackboard of the mind, and with it we can selectively "forget" issues that are important to discuss.

But the unconscious remembers. The unconscious gathers these rejected issues into its shadows and grows them strong and powerful in the darkness of our neglect.

Then if the unconscious is so mighty, how can we successfully change it?

Quite simply, with our old friend self-knowledge.

Once you meet your hidden demons, their strength begins to ebb. And the more you know about them, the more you take action against them, the weaker they become until at last they fade harmlessly into oblivion.

In this workbook you will find questions arranged in a series of self-tests. Taken together with the questions you've been answering throughout this book, these pragmatic self-tests not only will help you to concretize the unknowns and demons in your unconscious, they also will reveal a cumulative profile of your relationship as it is—and what to do to make it its intimate best.

As you answer the questions, you will create your own personal agenda for change, an agenda that will show you how to bring more and more intimacy into your life. By following your agenda, you can move out of the range of the unconscious and its diabolical shadows and into the clear light of consciousness with all its choices, freedom, and fulfillment.

In relationship workshops I have conducted throughout the country I have found that these self-tests are an invaluable conclusion to the theories that have been presented about intimacy. They require personal involvement in applying them to your own life. They ask the hard, sometimes painful questions that in much relationship counseling often escape direct confrontation.

In these self-tests you will be able to demonstrate your capacity for honesty in your relationship. Honest answers can cause the unhooking of the life-support system for a relationship that is already dead. But not one of the questions will cause an answer that will terminate a living relationship. Instead, your honesty will bring to the surface damage that is far more dangerous hidden than it is confronted, and in the healing of the damage your love can strengthen and grow.

SELF-TEST DIRECTIONS

To benefit most from this workbook, I recommend both you and your partner take all of the tests in the order given. (If your partner won't or can't participate, or if you have no partner, please take the tests alone. The more you know about yourself, the more effective you will be in achieving happiness.)

You can write on the pages provided in the workbook, or you can use your own paper.

The sample answers I've given for some of the questions are only to get you started. For your greatest enlightenment, don't censor or limit your thoughts when you read a question. Simply write down whatever comes into your mind as accurately and as fully as you can, and then go on to the next question.

Feel free to take mental rest periods whenever you grow tired. There are many questions, and each of them is important. Cumulatively they provide not only a revealing analysis of your unique relationship, they also offer concrete remedies for change.

When both of you have finished all of the questions, please begin discussion. Your perspective will be rounded by the addition of your partner's viewpoint, just as your partner's will be rounded by yours. Together you can confront your individual and mutual demons, and move into the warmth and light of lasting intimate love.

SELF-TEST 1

Intimacy

Describe the height of intimacy that you have experienced in the past. How did it feel? What did it look like? Give examples. (For further information, see Chapters 1 and 2.)

Describe intimacy as you experience it now. What does it look like? What does it feel like? Give examples.

Describe intimacy as you would like to experience it.

Describe the differences between intimacy as you experience it now, and intimacy as you would like to have it in your life.

This description of the differences is very important—and it's your first agenda for change.

SELF-TEST 2

Abandonment

Have you ever been abandoned in a relationship? Describe your experiences. (For more information on abandonment, see Chapters 3, 6, and 11.)

Have you ever abandoned another person in a relationship? What happened? What was it like? In your present relationship, what would cause you to abandon your partner? What do you think would cause your partner to abandon you?

Describe the difference between your relationship as you experience it now, and a relationship in which there was neither an outward threat nor an inward fear of abandonment.

The differences are very important—this is your second agenda for change.

SELF-TEST 3

Sabotage

How do you sabotage your intimate relationship? Do you use testing, broken promises, inappropriate expectations, etc.? Describe how your methods work. Give examples. (For more information, see Chapters 3 and 12.)

From your perspective, how does your partner sabotage your intimate relationship? Does he or she use testing, broken promises, inappropriate expectations, etc.? Describe how your partner's methods work. Give examples.

Describe the differences between the relationship you now experience and what you envision a sabotage-free relationship would be like.

This description is vital—it's your next agenda for change.

SELF-TEST 4

Intimacy Deprivation

List your symptoms of intimacy deprivation. Describe how they affect you. Remember, lack of intimacy is one of the major causes of distress and its symptoms. (For more information, see Chapters 5 and 7.)

Emotional symptoms (such as depression, anxiety, mood swings):

Physical symptoms (such as headaches, sexual dysfunction, ulcers):

Behavioral symptoms (such as binge eating or drinking, nervous smoking, overly aggressive behavior):

Describe what a revitalized relationship would do to alleviate each of the symptoms you've listed. For instance, are you identifying your depression, anxiety, smoking, drinking, migraines, or sexual dysfunction, etc. with your relationship to your partner? What would happen instead if your intimate relationship grew deeper, more fulfilling?

What causes distress in your relationship? For instance, do you funnel into the relationship negative energy from concerns about money, children, jobs, goals, sex, etc.? Give examples. (For more information, see Chapters 6, 7, 8, and 12.)

How do you deal with the distress in your relationship—listing both positive and negative methods? For instance, do you use communication, humor, hugging, or avoidance, denial, blame, anger, etc.? Give examples.

Describe the differences between your relationship as you experience it now, and your relationship as you envision its possibilities for being transforming and de-stressful.

These important differences give you your next agenda for change.

SELF-TEST 5

Power Games

How do you exercise power in your relationship? For instance, do you use sex, money, anger, sweetness, conflict, argument, violence, etc. to get what you want? How do you make your power games work? Give examples. (For more information, see Chapters 2, 3, and 9.)

From your perspective, how does your partner exercise power in your relationship? For instance, does your partner use sex, money, anger, sweetness, conflict, argument, violence, etc. to get what he or she wants? How does your partner make his or her power games work? Give examples.

Describe the differences between your relationship with its present power games, and what you envision your relationship would be if you and your partner cooperated in achieving your mutual happiness.

Here you have another important agenda for change.

SELF-TEST 6

Punishment

In your relationship, how do you punish your partner? For instance, do you use withdrawal, disdain, accusations, belittling, etc.? Give examples. (For more information, see Chapter 5.)

From your perspective, how does your partner punish you? For instance, does he or she use withdrawal, disdain, accusations, belittling, etc.? Give examples.

Describe the differences between your relationship as you experience it now, and a punishment-free relationship.

This is your next agenda for change.

SELF-TEST 7

Unmentionable Topics

What subjects or items can you not discuss with your partner? Give examples. (For more information, see Chapters 4 and 14.)

How do you avoid discussing these subjects or items? For instance, do you use lying, anger, passivity, putting the responsibility on others, etc.? Give examples.

What do you think the subjects or items are that your partner can *not* discuss with you? Give examples.

How does your partner avoid discussing these subjects or items? For instance, does he or she use lying, anger, passivity, putting the responsibility on others, etc.? Give examples.

Describe the differences between your relationship as you experience it now, and a relationship that you envision where any topic is welcome for discussion.

This is your next agenda for change.

SELF-TEST 8

Conflict

How do you deal with conflict in your relationship? For instance, do you use techniques of avoidance, of denial? Do you get angry, become fearful, etc.? Give examples. (For more information, please see Chapters 3 and 14.)

How does your partner deal with conflict in your relationship? Does your partner use techniques of avoidance, of denial? Get angry, become fearful, etc.? Give examples.

Describe the differences between the relationship you now have, and one that you envision in which conflict resolution offers opportunities for growth and coming closer together.

This is your next agenda for change.

SELF-TEST 9

Scripted Behaviors

What are the scripted behaviors through which your negative energy flows? (For more information, see Chapters 6, 7, and 12.)

YOUR BEHAVIORS

Verbal	Nonverbal
(for instance: loaded references, curses, name calling)	(for instance: eyeball rolling, withdrawal, sighing)

YOUR PARTNER'S BEHAVIORS

Verbal	Nonverbal

Compare your list with your partner's. What do you own and disown from your partner's list of *your* behaviors?

Describe the differences between your present relationship, and one that you can picture in which destructive, scripted behaviors are no longer a part of the life you and your partner share.

This is your agenda for change.

SELF-TEST 10

Circuit Breakers

What positive energy expressions do you bring as circuit breakers to conflicted moments in your relationship? For instance, do you use touching, allowing silence to happen, backing off, laughter, humor, saying "I love you," sometimes necessary confrontation— "I don't like what you're doing." Give examples. (For more information, see Chapters 6 and 9.)

What positive energy expressions does your partner bring as circuit breakers to conflicted moments in your relationship? For instance, does your partner use touching, allowing silence to happen, backing off, laughter, humor, saying "I love you," sometimes necessary confrontation— "I don't like what you're doing." Give examples. Which works best for you?

Describe the differences between your relationship as you experience it now, and one that you picture in which you and your partner use positive circuit breakers whenever negative, conflicted moments arise.

This is your next agenda for change.

SELF-TEST 11

Forgiveness

What do you need to forgive in your present relationship and in past relationships? Explain and describe. (For more information, see Chapter 14.)

For what do you need to be forgiven? Explain and describe.

Visualize yourself in situations in which you do the forgiving you
need to do, and are forgiven for that which you need forgiveness.
What does it look like? What does it feel like? Describe several
examples.

This agenda for change is vital; it can open a door through which
you can find peace.

SELF-TEST 12

The Words of Intimacy

In Chapter 16 we discussed the ever-widening dimensions of intimacy that can arise from simple, everyday interactions. Listed in the same order in which they appear in the chapter, here are the words describing those actions. Test yourself on how they apply to your relationship. For further explanation, you might like to reread that part of the chapter.

Do you *receive* the experience of these words? (Please write "yes" or "no.")	Do you *offer* the experience of these words? (Please write "yes" or "no.")
touching	
tenderness	
laughing	
crying	
talking	
silence	
giving	
receiving	
openness	
trust	
pain	
pleasure	
sexuality	

respect
_____
courtesy
_____
autonomy
_____
honesty
_____
faith
_____
apologies
_____
forgiveness
_____
surrender
_____
argument
_____
ideas
_____
promises
_____
expectations
_____
fidelity
_____
discipline
_____
priority
_____
commitment
_____
attitude
_____
specialness
_____
"I love you"
_____

The intimacy experiences that are missing from your relationship represent holes through which the life of your relationship can slip away and disappear. Add your own words to the list.

Visualize you and your partner in concrete experiences in

which you take turns successfully initiating the action of each intimacy word. Write a description of one of those experiences.

Describe the differences between your relationship as you experience it now, and what your relationship would be like if all of the words on the self-test list and on your own personal list were part of the day-to-day life of you and your partner.

SELF-TEST 13

Relationship Vibrancy

What can you contribute to the renewal of your relationship? What can your partner contribute? Give examples of the vibrancy of your relationship as you once experienced it, or of your relationship as you hope it might be. For instance, you might want wonderful sex, laughter, singing, traveling, sharing spiritual experiences, talking, walking, touching, holding hands, caressing, etc. List all of your desires; nothing is impossible. And no one but you and your partner can script what your relationship is like or should be like.

This description of your desires is a primary reason you have agenda for change. And now you have many tools to achieve them. I wish you much intimacy—and happiness.

SELF-TEST 14

Your Love Letter

On the next page, or on your own stationery, write a love letter to your partner—the significant other person in your relationship.

Tell him or her of your love. Describe what you can give to your partner so that your partner can recognize how primary he or she is to your life. Describe your vision of intimacy. Open up with your fears of abandonment, the ways in which you sabotage the relationship, how your commitment and priorities sometimes feel shaky. Share your intimate expectations for your relationship and the place it has in your life. Describe what you need to be forgiven for, what you would like to offer forgiveness for, and how you envisage asking for and giving forgiveness.

Write your love letter from your newfound knowledge, and from the strength of your belief in yourself and your future with your partner. Remember, you don't have to know how the future will turn out, only that you will work to attain a future that will bring you and your partner every possible happiness.

Intimacy is an on-going experience, not a statue on a pedestal. It is as alive as the two people who live it. By working together on your relationship, you have an excellent chance to live your life-time in fulfilling, happy intimacy.

My Love Letter

And now, one further act of love—
please deliver your letter.
(The end—or could it be the beginning?)